A Small Piece of Pure Gold

To Jane

Best wishes

A Small Piece of Pure Gold

Jack McGinnigle

John Nodding

Jack McGinnigle

and

John Nodding

Highland

First published in 2015 by Highland Books Ltd, 2 High Pines, Knoll Road, Godalming, Surrey, GU7 2EP.

Cover design by Helen Nodding

ISBN-13: 978-1897913-92-5

ISBN-10: 1-897913-92-3

e-edition ISBN: 978-1909690-92-9

Printed in Great Britain by CPI Anthony Rowe.

Contents

Dedication

John, Maureen, Paul, Mark and Helen

John

It was not long after I moved my home to the Midlands of England that I first met John Nodding in the Methodist Church nearest to my new house. I spotted John right away as a "major player" in that church. (All churches have "major players", just as in life everywhere else!) Looking across the room, I saw a man in robust middle age, tall, well-made and with a slightly surprising shock of pure white wavy hair; an unmissable figure as he chatted easily to all around him, constantly smiling and animated. I soon found out that he was the "Senior Circuit Steward" at that time, a very important lay position in the administration of any Circuit (group) of Methodist Churches.

We soon met and a firm friendship developed, made all the stronger when we both exercised at the same gym – for both of us, a consequence of irritating cardiac problems. At these times, many a weighty discussion took place on adjacent exercise cycles or rowing machines!

This book is John's story as told to me. It is filled with all the love, joy, sadness and tragedy that is a part of human life on our wonderful planet. It has been a great pleasure for me to write this book.

Jack McGinnigle

1

August, 2014

'**M**r Nodding, I think you've got motor neurone disease.'

These were the devastating words that my doctor uttered as we sat in his consulting room. This was just an ordinary doctor-patient consultation like so many before it – but now it had been completely transformed by the introduction of an absolute nightmare.

I said nothing but my reply to myself was abundantly clear, the words resonating within my heAD:

'NO! HE'S GOT THAT ALL WRONG.'

In fairness to my doctor, his words were a necessary response to a direct question of mine. Before this crucial exchange, I had heard the results of all the tests I had undergone in the weeks before. These were tests arranged as a result of a previous visit to the medical practice. The Computed Tomography (CT) scan had revealed nothing untoward, I had just been told. The same was true of the other x-ray images that had been taken. And, finally, none of the battery of tests that had been carried out on my blood samples had revealed any abnormal values.

'All is fine here', had been my doctor's welcome message. Sweet music to my ears!

However, it was in response to all this positive information that I had asked the fateful question:

'So why is my voice changing?' In previous weeks, I had become aware that my voice was weaker and distinctly more husky; also, I noticed that I was having occasional articulation difficulties with more complex words. In the past, I had never suffered from such problems.

My presence in the doctor's consulting room was the culmination of unfocussed feelings that something was not quite right. Even nine months before, family members had commented that I had "changed". These comments had been made by my son, Paul and also by our lifelong family friend, Diane. Both said that I seemed to have "slowed down" to some degree; furthermore, these comments continued to be made with increasing frequency in the subsequent months.

'Well, what do you expect?' My rejoinder was made with bravado and a certain degree of irritation, 'I'm 69 now, so I'm bound to be changing to some degree.'

In fact, I knew I had already changed in another fundamental, physical way. For many years, my weight had been steady at around 85 kilograms (kg). Now it had altered. For some time, my weight had been falling steadily and I had become increasingly aware of my changing body shape – perhaps something to be welcomed at first! However, when I eventually visited my doctor, I recognised that I had lost around 14kg, without any change in diet or lifestyle.

There was another significant event. In March 2014, I had a rather nasty accident – a rather dramatic and injurious fall. I was in the pleasant but very hilly city of Birmingham, (in the Midlands area of England) carrying out some financial duties at the Museum and Art Gallery, where I had been engaged to do some accountancy work.

A Small Piece of Pure Gold

The Birmingham Museum and Art Gallery is at the top of a majestic hill in the city and I was making rapid progress down one of the rather steep roads towards the railway station when I tripped and fell heavily, suffering serious bruising and acquiring a nasty wound on my forehead. People, including a passing doctor, were very kind and rushed to help me. An ambulance was called and I soon found myself in the Accident and Emergency Department of one of the city's hospitals. Although my accident was very unpleasant, with painful consequences for several weeks after, I blamed myself for not taking enough care.

'In the future, I'll watch out for uneven and ridged pavements,' I thought, 'and I'll try to remember I'm not a teenager! There's always the next train to catch. All this was all my own fault.'

So the evidence was mounting but we all have a tendency to minimise problems – I know I do, anyway! Even when we begin to suspect that something may be wrong with us, we refute it. 'It's just my imagination,' we cry. 'It's advancing age (though we don't believe that for a moment!) It's something I've eaten or drunk. Maybe I been overdoing things, etc., etc.' Then there comes a time when we decide we should act and seek advice. The spur for this can occur in many ways – in my case it was when I was approached by one of the nursing staff at the excellent "Heartcare" gym that I attend. She took me aside and told me that she was worried about me. She said she had noted my weight loss, my "slowing down" and the change to my voice. She thought I should consult my doctor about these changes.

This was the stimulus I had been waiting for. I decided to take her advice.

As I left the doctor's surgery after the consultation, I felt very shocked and disquieted – but I retained my staunch conviction that his suggested diagnosis was completely wrong. 'After all, they do get it wrong at times, don't they?

I've heard about wrong diagnoses many times …' However, try as I might, I couldn't think of a single example at that time!

Of course, the doctor's "bombshell" diagnosis had not been the end of the consultation. He went on to advise me that the next step was to be examined by a consultant neurologist, a specialist in such conditions. The necessary paperwork would be completed immediately, he said, so that the visit to the specialist would happen as soon as possible. In the event, I was able to arrange an early appointment with the designated consultant neurologist. 'The sooner the better,' I decided. 'Let's have this diagnosis of motor neurone disease (MND) quashed! Let's get me started on treatment for whatever problem my sixty-nine year-old body has developed.' I remained resolute and convinced that my problem was likely to be caused by some minor imbalance.

My visit to the consultant neurologist involved a very thorough examination during which I had to undress almost completely and have most parts of my anatomy poked, prodded and twisted. In addition, I was required to demonstrate the extent of my strength, flexibility and coordination by carrying out various physical movements while he watched me carefully. It was not a pleasant experience but I knew it had to be done. He asked very many questions about my lifestyle, past and present. On hearing about the accident in Birmingham, he opined that it was very likely to be part of the range of symptoms associated with the medical problem he was now investigating.

At the end of the examination, the neurologist advised me that more tests were required and that he wanted me to have a Magnetic Resonance Imaging (MRI) brain and neck scan. He also told me he was referring me to another consultant for nerve conduction studies; this would involve special reaction tests on a range of nerves and muscles, using electrodes and needles. This specialist, a clinical neurophysiologist, was one of only a handful of doctors in the UK who carried out such tests, he told me. This would provide valuable information for the diagnosis, he said. I understood that the purpose of the tests was to discover the extent of nerve injury and to assess the degree of possible recovery that could be expected.

The visit to the second specialist proved to be an even more uncomfortable experience. As explained by the neurologist, the stimulation of my nerves and muscles was either by electric current or sharp needles. When this was being done, every time I reacted to the stimulations (as I often did), I noted that the consultant apologised: 'Sorry!' he said each time.

'Why do you say "sorry" every time I react?' I asked him.

'Well,' he replied, 'I know that I'm hurting you, and I'm sorry for that. However, it's the only way we have of discovering the truth.'

THE TRUTH. These two words were welcome, indeed. 'Ah yes,' I remember thinking, 'that's why I'm here; to discover THE TRUTH. To get rid of this MND suggestion and to discover the solution to whatever problem is responsible for my symptoms. I certainly look forward to returning to full health and strength.' That thought made me feel happy and filled me with a surge of welcome optimism! Eventually, the examination was over. Now I concentrated upon this man who was setting aside the various instruments he had been using on me. My gaze was fixed directly upon him. Here was the man who would tell me "the truth". I waited. And waited. The silence in the room lengthened but, still, he said nothing. His head was down as he examined the various readings that his equipment had presented to him. Eventually, I felt it was appropriate to break the silence; to move things forward:

'So am I all right?' This was my brief, direct question. I felt quite upbeat as I spoke these words.

'No,' he replied immediately, his voice quiet and flat.

I froze, recognising in that moment that my world, my life, had changed. That was the moment that I said to myself: 'I really have got MND.' I couldn't refute it any longer.

On my return visit to the first specialist, I was informed that the MRI scan had not revealed anything of significance and the report of the nerve conduction studies from the second specialist had ruled out several possible diseases and disorders. Crucially, however, it did not rule out MND and it was the neurophysiologist's opinion, and the opinion of my neurologist, that MND was indeed the diagnosis of my condition. The neurologist communicated this diagnosis to me carefully and comprehensively; then, in his follow-up letter to my doctor (copied to me), he wrote:

> "I have explained to Mr Nodding that I do consider he has motor neurone disease."

An unequivocal statement indeed. Now it was confirmed positively that my status had changed irrevocably. My neurologist advised me that I would be referred, as an MND sufferer, to the New Queen Elizabeth Hospital at Edgbaston, Birmingham. This is an ultra-modern, premier hospital known to be in the forefront of many present day medical techniques. It is also well known across the UK as the hospital that treats the serious casualties of war who return from conflict, often with devastating injuries. Within the Department of Neurosciences of this hospital, there is a Motor Neurone Disease Care Centre, led by leading specialists in the disease.

Until now, everything had been happening very quickly, almost at breakneck speed. The diagnosis of MND had been established very quickly, despite the range of consultations that I needed to have with different specialists.

Consequently, I was disappointed that a nine-week delay now occurred before contact with the MND Care Centre team was established. This was very worrying, because I noted that my condition continued to deteriorate.

However, when action began to happen, it was like the deployment of the support troops! Firstly, I was visited in my home by a delightful specialist nurse from the MND Care Centre. The nurse painted for me a very detailed picture of MND, explaining that it is a progressive disease that attacks the "motor neurones" (nerves) of the brain and those within the spinal cord. The result is progressive weakness and wasting. At present, there is no cure but symptoms are managed so that the best quality of life may be achieved for each sufferer. She emphasised that the course of the disease is different for each patient; it is impossible to predict how it will run its course in any individual, she said. This was an excellent introduction to how my life would change in the future and I was very grateful for all the information that was given to me during the specialist nurse's visit.

Soon after, I was also visited by an expert from the MND Association, which is a charity organisation operating across England, Wales and Northern Ireland. This organisation funds MND research, campaigns to raise awareness of the disease and has thousands of trained staff and volunteers in many centres to support the sufferers of MND and their families. In Birmingham, the MND Association staff work with the MND Care Centre at the Queen Elizabeth Hospital. During this visit, I received expert advice on how I might change my house, specifically how to change the downstairs bathroom into a "wet room" and transfer all my living quarters to be solely on the ground floor. I was advised that the Association has practical contacts with specialist companies who can carry out conversion work at favourable rates to the client. There was also a medical discussion about the provision of an external feeding tube to the stomach if food cannot be taken via the throat.

I was also briefed on other aspects of MND care in the area. There is a team from a local hospice (the John Taylor Hospice, who have been offering end-of-life care for over 100 years) who concentrate on MND patients, providing various therapies, including advice and treatment on nutrition and physiotherapy aspects of care. Furthermore, a Speech and Language Therapist is available within the Birmingham Community Healthcare system, while advice on respiratory care is available within another function at the Queen Elizabeth hospital. All this information was very helpful and I am most grateful that so many comprehensive services are available to help me.

At time of writing this account, work is being done to convert my house, so that it will be suitable for my physical state in the future and make me as comfortable as possible. Friends and family are helping with this. Items that I will soon need (e.g. a wheelchair) will be delivered to me in due course.

Meanwhile, I am still losing weight through the wasting of my muscles and consequently becoming weaker. I find I have little energy and stamina. This also affects my mind and I am finding it more and more difficult to concentrate.

My world is changing; where I have been helping others, people are now helping me.

Three months have passed. Now it is November and I think back about my life; about the good and the not-so-good things that have happened to me during my seventy years in this wonderful world. I think about the great joys there have been in my life and I think about the sorrows, too.

That's what the rest of this book is about.

2

My Beginning

I have always joked that "I was born within the smell of the gasworks", a wry comparison with the proud Cockney London claim of being "born within earshot of the famous Bow Bells." The gasworks to which I refer were in the suburb of Nechells, Birmingham. In 1944, the gas supply to the population of the UK was "coal gas", the generation of which caused a characteristic and all-pervading smell of gas around the site where the gas was produced by burning coal. Traditionally, the generated gas was stored in enormous metal gasholders that were adjacent to the gas generation works. In Nechells, there were two of these huge, inverted, cylindrical steel tanks that rose up from the ground within a supporting framework of girders, as the volume of gas collected and was compressed inside. Then, as the population used the gas, the gasholder tanks sank back into the ground. Virtually every population centre of any size had gasworks with their accompanying characteristic smell. Of course, for many years now, the modern gas supply is not generated locally but piped in from elsewhere. Additionally, it is no longer coal gas and is odourless; however, for safety, a "gas smell" is added.

In fact, the part of Nechells into which I was born in 1944 was a distinctly grim place. There was poverty, deprivation and all the ills that are associated with such circumstances. The houses were old, small and generally in poor repair. Of course, they lacked the facilities we take for granted today. My parents' house in St. Clements Road, was of typical size and condition but made worse by the fact that the front room had been converted into a small shop, which was overseen by my mother. This meant that, although the shop contributed financially to the family, the living space in the house was severely reduced.

So in October 1944, I arrived into this world, no doubt to the accompanying smell of gas! I was number two in the birth agenda of that day, because I appeared one and a half hours after the birth of my "big" twin brother, Gerald. I have been told that my mother was confident that she would give birth to twins but the family doctor had disagreed, insisting that there was only one baby in the womb. On the day of the birth, it is said that the doctor delivered Gerald and then admitted to my mother – "You're right!" – as he identified that a further birth (me!) was due to take place.

Thus, Gerald and I joined the only other child in the family, David, who had been born in the previous year. (There had also been two early infant deaths in the family, in 1942 and again in 1943.) We were not identical twins but, with rather similar hair and eye colour, we were thought to be quite alike, especially as young children.

Although our family lived in the same highly restricted conditions as the rest of the people of this part of Nechells, there was obviously a powerful spirit of commerce at work within my parents and their other social activities (to be explained later on) suggested that they were far from typical of the general population of the area.

My father Bernard came from the small village community of Cockfield in County Durham, England. On leaving school at the age of fourteen (the earliest school leaving age in the far distant days of 1923), he soon busied himself with a personal enterprise – selling fruit and vegetables around the village from a handcart. Later, he graduated to a larger cart, pulled by a horse and, later still, to an elderly van. This continued something of a tradition in the family; although his father worked as a coal miner all his life, his mother had been a shopkeeper in the village.

This mention of my paternal grandparents brings to mind the memory of a significant incident in my life. I have very few direct memories of my grandparents; however, this one is special and retained in my mind. As a young boy, these were the only grandparents I knew. They lived in a village house that was typical of the times. I well remember that the "facilities" were situated at the very end of their back garden, which was the norm for such houses. This memory is retained for a very good reason. The small shed contained a very basic dry earth toilet. On this occasion, I had visited the toilet, clutching, for some unknown reason, a florin in my hand. (For the modern reader, a florin is a large silver coin worth two shillings, equal to a mere 10 pence today.) This was a significant amount of money in those days, especially for a young boy! Tragically, while making use of the toilet, I managed to drop this very valuable coin into its depths! I can remember looking down through the circular hole with great sadness, knowing with certainty that my wonderful coin had gone forever! Obviously, this was a significant event in my life, so catastrophic that it remains vivid in my memory to this day!

However, I must now return to the story of my father and the wife he had yet to meet. Bernard's business took him to the villages surrounding Cockfield where he continued to sell fruit and vegetables from his van. One of these was Ingleton, a small village a mere 5 miles or so away. It was in the village of Ingleton that Bernard came into contact with a bright and talented young lady called Mary Allsop. She had been born and brought up in Ingleton, where her family were comfortably off; also, they were regular attendees at the Methodist Chapel in the village. Bernard and Mary fell in love and eventually married in the village Methodist Chapel in 1941.

As I grew to adulthood, I was puzzled by the story of my mother and father's union. Why would a bright, intelligent and well-off young Christian lady choose to marry a relatively uneducated man who sold vegetables from an old, shabby greengrocer's van? On the face of it, it would seem that their social circumstances were very widely separated. I was sure that the wide variation in the circumstances of Bernard and Mary would be of great significance in those days, especially in the close confines of rural village life. Of course I know that in human romances, such surprising and unexpected things do happen but still, it rather mystified me. Then, only recently, I learned the truth from an elderly aunt. It is a story of some complexity and it proved to be revelation for me.

In 1935, when Bernard was twenty-six, he was directly involved in a dreadful tragedy in his village – an event that had dreadful consequences for him. One day, while his van was parked by the roadside, a one-year old child crawled unnoticed under the vehicle. Shortly after, when Bernard returned to his vehicle and drove away, the child was killed instantly under its wheels. Bernard was completely devastated and, in his sorrow and remorse, became deeply depressed. This was only the start of his problems, however. It would seem that the village blamed him directly for the infant's death, although there was no way he could have suspected that a small child would have crawled beneath his vehicle. He became deeply unpopular and his business suffered badly. His sadness and hurt for the injustice of it all deepened his depression further.

He may never have recovered from this tragedy had it not been for the intervention of a Christian friend. Aware

A Small Piece of Pure Gold

of all that was happening, this young man sought Bernard out inform him that he was soon to leave Cockfield to study at Cliff College, a Methodist evangelical Bible college located at Calver in Derbyshire. He told Bernard earnestly that he wanted to take him with him to this college. Ostracised, bitter and distressed, Bernard agreed and, subsequently, they both studied there for three years, eventually becoming accredited and commissioned as Local Preachers in the Methodist Church.

Cliff College was set up in the 19th Century and has been in existence at Calver for well over 100 years. Historically, the College operated as a training facility for lay preachers but, today, the courses are considerably more extensive and diverse to meet the needs of the modern Christian world. However, it is to be noted that most services in today's Methodist churches are still led by lay preachers (traditionally still designated Local Preachers) who have completed rigorous training to become fully accredited and commissioned to that office. Today, a fully accredited Local Preacher is authorised to preach in any Methodist church in the world, despite the rather confusing "Local" designation. In fact, "Local" refers only to the fact that these preachers are not "posted" around the country like the ordained ministers (presbyters) of the Methodist Church.

Thus, the 29 year-old Bernard appeared to Mary Allsop in Ingleton, not as an uneducated man selling fruit and vegetables from an old van but as a college-educated Christian businessman who was an accredited Local Preacher of the Methodist Church, a position that commanded significant respect. It is imagined that Mary's parents, staunch Methodists themselves, would be content when it transpired that their daughter was marrying such an important man!

Little is known about my father and mother's life in the years around the time of their marriage in 1941. However, Bernard obviously decided that his life was untenable in the area of his birth; no doubt the infant tragedy played a part in that decision. In fact I believe that Bernard never returned to his home village. Instead, he sought his fortune in the city of Birmingham and he always insisted that he arrived in the city with a mere three shillings (15p) in his pocket. It is assumed he had moved there alone, before the time of his marriage and, subsequently, was joined by his wife in 1941. The Noddings set up their home in the Birmingham suburb of Nechells, in the modest house fronted by the shop that I have described earlier.

Meanwhile, the Second World War was in progress but, because my father was a member of the Fire Service of the area, he did not serve in the Armed Forces. By 1946, the family had been expanded again by the arrival of my sister Angela and our family home moved to a much more spacious house in Erdington (another suburb of Birmingham). My father had been able to buy two adjacent shops with living accommodation above and our house occupied the two floors above the family shop. The other shop and the accommodation above and behind were rented out by my father. In addition, there were other buildings behind the house plus a very long and narrow strip of land. An open access between the shops was wide enough for vehicles; this meant that there was ample space for my father to develop the family fruit and vegetable business, which he did in subsequent years. However, as a small child, I do remember that one of the tenants kept a horse in one of the back yard outhouses!

In 1950, our family expanded for a final time, when my brother Peter was born.

There is one final twist in the story of my mother and father. As a young lady, my mother Mary was an impressive, intelligent and distinctly flamboyant person with acting ambitions. In fact I understood that she successfully auditioned for a Birmingham theatre company, being offered a place in the company as an actress. However, family restraints prevented her from accepting this position and following an acting career. As a result, she decided to follow her husband's example and become a Local Preacher in the Methodist Church, an ambition she achieved after the necessary period of study and training. Thwarted from becoming a flamboyant actress, she became a flamboyant Methodist preacher!

Thus, both my parents were highly active in the Methodist churches of the surrounding area. Obviously, from a very early age, all the Nodding children became "devout" churchgoers, including me.

3

Love One Another...

"Love one another. As I have loved
you, so you must love one another."

(The Holy Bible, New International Version, 1973).
One translation of the words of Jesus Christ; a
Christian command of great importance.

'**D**id you have a happy childhood?'

I know lots of people who would answer "Yes" to that question. Quite a few would answer it more fulsomely, e.g. "Very happy!", "Wonderful!", "Marvellous!", etc. Then, details of the "very happy" childhood would follow. However, close questioning would normally reveal that there were times of naughtiness or even bad behaviour (very rare, of course!) that resulted in reprimand or even punishment of some kind. We all know that no specimen of humanity, however winsome and attractive, is perfect! Admitting to those imperfections, my respondents would sometimes qualify their responses, perhaps adding: '... apart from the (very) few times I got into trouble over...'

On the other hand, the same question put to some others would result in a pause and a darkening of demeanour. Eventually, they would answer: "No, I didn't", usually in a downbeat, low voice. Sometimes, the answers would be expressed more equivocally, perhaps spoken in a sad, wry tone: "Not really", "Not very often", etc. Furthermore, the person who answers "No" will often be reluctant to talk about their early childhood experiences; embarrassed, even. If detail is given, the specific reasons and circumstances for the unhappiness, deprivation and punishment are likely to be vastly different in each case. Deprivation and punishment may take many forms but all cause unhappiness and worse.

Personally, I find it very difficult to answer the question about a happy childhood. Clearly, the Nodding family, two adults and (eventually) five children, were devout Christians. Both my mother and my father were Christian teachers and leaders of worship, a responsibility they carried out at a range of Methodist churches in the Birmingham area. As such, they were very highly respected in all the communities where they were known. In addition, my father was a Prison Visitor, who was so trusted in this role that he held his own key to Winston Green Prison in Birmingham. I understand that he was held in no little affection by some of the prisoners there, who painted pictures or made models as gifts for him. He also devoted considerable time to families whose lives were being destroyed by alcohol consumption, visiting them in their homes and attempting to help them recover from their devastating addiction. There is no doubt that my father did a considerable amount of good work in the community.

Of course, all the Nodding children were required to be regular churchgoers, attending the large Methodist Church in Stockland Green, a suburb of Birmingham not far from the family home. The children attended three times on each Sunday: Morning Service at 11.00 a.m., Sunday School at 3.00 p.m. and the Evening Service at 6.30 p.m. All this would suggest that our family would be totally devoted Christians, filled with the love and joy of Christ. This was what my mother and father taught in their preaching. This is what my father brought to his other ministries in the community. This is what the Nodding children were taught at Church and in the Sunday School.

Regrettably, I cannot say that I ever found much of the joy and love of Christ in my home life. On the other hand, neither can I say that I, or any of my brothers and sister were deprived. We were fed, clothed and well looked after but both my mother and father were always very busy working hard – so hard, it would seem, that they had little time for, or interest in, their children. It will be recalled that my mother ran the family shop that was located on the ground floor of our premises. I remember that she worked there constantly and was generally not available to her children. Likewise, my father was always engaged in his business, entrepreneurial activities or other charity work. Apart from his preaching, his pastoral work in the prison or with alcoholic families, his major focus seemed to be the development of his business to improve his and the family's situation in life. While all this may appear to be admirable, I have to say it was carried out without discernible affection towards his family.

My father's dealings with his children tended to be harsh. I do not remember him having any interest in Gerald and me when we were young boys; at this stage. I think he generally ignored us. Things changed as we reached an age when we were strong enough to carry out work in the family business; I recall this happening around the age of twelve or so. From then on, he would berate us strongly every time he found us reading a book or any other publication. 'Stop wasting your time with that,' he would roar bitterly (there was always a good deal of shouting in our house), 'there's work to be done.' Then he would order us to carry out tasks in the shop or storerooms in the yard behind the house. This was often heavy, tiring, physical work. This was our situation throughout our lives as boys and a teenagers. When we worked for our father, we were never paid or even thanked. As far as we could see, he thought of Gerald and me as his slaves. For our part, we were always afraid of him and dreaded his presence in the house.

Then there was the ritual of Sunday lunch, vividly remembered, when all the family shared a meal around a large table. This was, in fact, far from the traditional family ritual, defined as the sharing of a meal together in a spirit of joy and love. On every occasion, there was one topic of discussion during Sunday lunch and that was the content of the sermon that had been preached at church that morning, a couple of hours before. This would be discussed in great detail by my mother and father. During the whole of this discussion, which on each occasion lasted throughout the meal, the children were forbidden to speak. If they did, they would be punished, traditionally by "sending to bed", with hard slaps to face or body sometimes added for good measure. Sunday lunch was, of course, a thoroughly unpleasant and oppressive time, universally hated by me and my brothers and sister.

Although we were never subjected to beatings, stinging slaps to the head and other exposed parts of our bodies were quite common, administered for quite minor offences. Such punishments could happen most unexpectedly. I remember making a rather puerile joke about a baptism that my mother was talking about (I have to admit that this was at the hallowed Sunday Lunch table!) and receiving from her a very powerful and ringing slap to the head for this serious misdemeanour. It bewildered me, because I was only trying to amuse, I have always claimed. (However, yes, I do agree that there was also an element of rebellion in my action! No doubt my mother was aware of this.)

Of course, as a child, I coped with the verbal and physical attacks as part of my life. In truth, I recognise that some of the punishments were justified. However, in more mature adulthood, I do think that the behaviour of my parents towards their children was hardly in the Christian spirit that they seemed to advocate in all other circumstances. To this day, this does disappoint and perplex me.

So, in the middle of all this, what were we Nodding children like? The answer is: we were generally pretty aggressive! It is a fact that violence begets violence and there was a good deal of serious physical fighting between David, Gerald and I. Of course, Gerald and I were twins and we did have an underlying bond of friendship (yet we fought violently!). Deep down, I think we were good friends who would support each other in times of trouble. I admired Gerald. I recognised that he was more athletic and "sporty" than I, while I believe I was physically more powerful than him and, I think, more aggressive! Inside, however, I was very shy and rather timid while Gerald was confident and highly articulate. He could be devastatingly acerbic and did not hesitate to use this weapon with skill – and sometimes against me!

Very young children have few early recollections of their lives and I am no exception. I remember attending a playgroup with Gerald when I was three or four years old. I recall an enjoyable experience but no significant detail. Somewhat older, I remember playing games in the street with many other children, no doubt all the usual range of ball games. I recall hopscotch, too. Children playing in the street was very much the norm in those days when road traffic was very sparse. It is, of course, unimaginable now in any road where there is through traffic.

From where I lived, a large public park was a short distance away and the children went to play there also. I have particularly enjoyable memories of fishing in the large lake there – a very popular activity for all the youngsters. We would arrive there with small fishing nets on poles and empty jam jars at the ready. After some hours, we returned home triumphantly (sometimes!) with several, unfortunate, tiny fish swimming around in our water-filled jars. We would then have the fascination of watching the behaviour of these small creatures in our bedrooms. Of course, away from their environment, they did not survive for long. As a child, I had been told that these little fish were "gudgeons"; when I was older, I identified gudgeons as small freshwater fish that tended to live near the bottom of ponds and streams, so it seemed that my earlier information was likely to be correct.

There were other exciting childhood occasions when older boys constructed wheeled carts from scrap wooden boxes, planks and old pram wheels. These ramshackle vehicles were then taken to places where there were steep hills. I remember the excitement of seeing these dangerous vehicles racing down the hills, precariously guided by older boys. Occasionally, I was allowed to board one (if my courage was sufficient!), and remember the exhilarating speed, the wind in my face and the "end of roller-coaster ride" relief when I survived the event. However, I also recall the sight and the personal pain of cuts, bruises and scrapes when these very dangerous vehicles crashed at speed, which they frequently did!

Another major influence in my life was becoming an enthusiastic member of the Cub Pack that was associated with the Stockland Green Methodist Church (The 253rd Pack). At the age of eight, Gerald and I both attended regularly. Of course, the Cub Pack was focussed on learning a whole range of skills. Just like today, proficiency in a skill meant that you were awarded a badge, which was then sewn on to your uniform. The largest possible range of proficiency badges was the ambition of every Cub! In addition, Cubs were formed into groups of six, commanded by a "Sixer", who had a "Seconder" as a second-in-command. While I did manage to become a Seconder, my impressive brother Gerald rose to the exalted rank of Sixer! Finally, when a Cub reaches the age of 11, they transfer to the Boy Scouts and the whole process of badge acquiring starts again. This is also around the time that the process of becoming an adult begins!

Schooling is a very major component in the life of any child. Gerald and I attended a nearby school from the age of five, where we were placed in the same class during our time in junior school. In those days, it seems that the norm was to place twins in the same class. While there are always sets of twins in every school, our junior school was considered exceptional, having no less than eleven sets of twins within its pupil total!

Basically, I liked school and I liked learning. I was largely successful at the subjects I was taught there. All that would have made for a happy and contented segment of my daily life were it not for an unfortunate personal development, which afflicted me throughout my schooling and greatly affected my confidence.

It is a characteristic of human nature to present ourselves to others in the best light possible. Basically, this means that we conceal our problems, be they physical, psychological or both. We desperately seek normality and conformity. Especially when we are young, we seek to be just like all the well-balanced, happy and contented children around us, knowing with certainty that every one of them has absolutely no problems of any kind. No pain, no discomfort, no worries, etc. Nothing to spoil their perfect lives. Of course, the fact that we are surrounded by serene, happy individuals with no problems has the effect of exacerbating our own personal problems. Even when we apply logic to the situation and *know* that every other person cannot be problem-free, our emotions will not allow us to accept this, especially if we are young and inexperienced in life. This was precisely my situation.

My problem was simple. It seems that my young body required me to visit the toilet in the mid-morning, in fact, very soon after the 9 o'clock bell signalled the start of school classes. I observed that none of the other children needed to do this – they were seen by me to be examples of perfection in this matter! In the first two years of my schooling, this was not a problem; permission was given and the visit made without problem. However, the situation worsened as I grew older. Teachers could be unsympathetic when my request to leave was made. However, in any event, my necessity to leave was always acutely embarrassing for me. Of course there were many occasions when I fought the physical need and this was of course greatly uncomfortable. Sometimes, observing my discomfort, my brother Gerald would seek permission for me to leave, to general hilarity within the class!

Of course, I accept that there was not only a physical element here but a psychological one too. I eventually grew out of it, but it is a good example of the extreme sensitivity of a human being. Already quiet and shy before I went to school, this made my shyness much worse and affected my life materially. At my young age, there was no way I could understand either the degree of complexity and sensitivity that is a part of humanity or come to terms with the reality of the complex behavioural rules that society foists upon us all. I think that my story (and the secret, unknown myriads of other people's stories like it) should be borne in mind by us all.

There are always two sides to a coin, however. In the midst of the worry, discomfort and cruelty that is present in my story above, there was also a lovely example of affection, which I must include here. During that agonising time for me, an attractive little girl who attended my church approached me at Sunday School and told me that she was the "Organiser of my Fan Club"! (Fan Clubs were very popular in those days.) Having stated this, she then promoted my "image" within the church community and everywhere else whenever the opportunity arose. I was very grateful then – and surprised, too. Now, I think that what she did was an act of amazing love.

Earlier in this chapter, I mentioned my "promotion" from the Cubs to the Scouts and how this is often coincident with the beginning of the development of more adult desires. This is similarly true of the female organisation of the Scouting movement, when a girl progresses to the Girl Guides. I think that I was always attracted to the opposite sex, although, as a young boy, not of course in any adult way. I recall thinking that, in general, girls were pleasant, kind and attractive to me in my earlier life. Many of the Scouts (including me) now found that they were attracted anew to the opposite sex and it seemed that, in some cases at least, the attraction was reciprocated. I recall in particular a young lady in the Guides (name not supplied here!) to whom I was attracted and I remember we became friends. I can say here that I now recall her with particular affection, because I recognise that she was the person who first showed me the joy of innocent love plus a wonderful example of the affection that appeared to have been deficient in my childhood.

I finish this chapter about my boyhood with two final pieces of information about me:

When I was six years old, I wanted to be thirteen. Why?

So that I could buy fireworks!

When I was thirteen, I wanted to be twenty-one. Why?

I'll leave you to work that one out!

4

Teenage Turbulence!

As I became an "established" teenager, the Scouts remained an important influence in my life. I was happy with the leadership, the teaching, the comradeship and the morality that I found there. It was in the Scouts that I discovered I had a talent for story-telling. Periodically, our Scout Troop would go camping in the countryside and I always found this to be a most enjoyable and relaxing time in my life, divorced from the stresses and strains that were so much a feature of my home environment. Sitting around a roaring campfire with my friends, I suddenly found that I was able to tell stories that were entertaining to my companions. All my Scouting friends sat around and listened with rapt attention – or so it seemed to me, anyway! These were in no way "formal" stories (i.e. written and published by someone else): they were just stories that I made up at the time, often filled with amusing aspects and twists. I also told jokes at other times and these seemed to be appreciated by all my friends. Although I knew that this was a talent I had somehow acquired in the middle of the acute shyness that dominated my "normal" life, I do not remember giving this phenomena any further thought. Nowadays, when I think back, I think it was an incredible thing to happen and I recognise it as a special God-given gift.

I have one other important memory from my Scouting days. As I have already mentioned earlier, every Scout has a burning desire to acquire as many Proficiency Badges as possible; these are then stitched on to the Scout uniform and thus are on permanent display, not only to fellow Scouts but to the general public at large. At a slightly older age, perhaps around 15-16, my lifelong friend Bob (we had been friends from the age of two!) became determined to acquire a "Hiker" badge. This involved finding your way around a designated, lengthy hiking route. To achieve this, he had to be accompanied by another Scout, as a process of certification. Bob was allowed to propose someone for this important role; he chose me and I accepted, of course. I well remember the day; we set off in high spirits and made excellent progress.

At one point our route took us across a large field in the countryside which was obviously used for large animals. When we entered the field through the gate, we did not notice that there was a continuous electric fence around the field, obviously to control the large animals who occupied it at times. It was when we reached the other side of the field and were about to climb over the fencing there that we noticed the electric wires strung between insulators in the fencing. Of course, we knew that such defences are not always in operative mode but the only way of finding that out is by touching the wires! We were also aware that the strength of the electric current in such systems has to be sufficient to repel large animals (cows, BULLS!), so it needs to be considerable. (At the thought of bulls, we looked around anxiously! Thankfully, there were none to be seen.)

Now I have mentioned before that, as a boy, I suffered from a significant degree of timidity and this situation was more than enough to bring it to the fore! I turned to Bob and spoke decisively:

A Small Piece of Pure Gold

'We can't risk it, Bob,' I said. 'It's too dangerous. We'll have to give up.' I was adamant. This has got to be the sensible thing to do, I thought. While climbing over this fearsome, totally terrifying electric fence, one or other of us would surely touch a wire and suffer a *severe electric shock.* That would be *extremely painful,* I thought, tremulously. We might be *seriously injured.* We might even be *KILLED!!*

'We can't risk it, Bob, we'll have to give up,' I repeated. Sadly, there was no other choice.

Bob said nothing as he stood with narrowed eyes, looking at the fence as if it was his worst enemy. Then his eyes swivelled around to look at me, knowing that my presence with him was essential. It was a frozen tableau for a moment until, wordlessly, he strode over to me, seized me with powerful arms, lifted me high above the ground and threw me bodily over the fence to land in the soft grass on the other side. Then he climbed over the fence, carefully avoiding the electric wires.

We continued our hike without further comment.

Subsequently, Bob was awarded his "Hiker" badge. I was very glad I hadn't let him down and was extremely grateful for his decisiveness and strength when confronted with a serious problem!

Of course, another "important influence" in my life was the Church. From my early teens, I was very active in the Church's internal organisations, for instance taking on the position of Treasurer of the Sunday School and, when required, carrying out other administrative tasks connected with the young people of the Church. It was around this time that something very important and significant happened to me. Quite suddenly – for the very first time – I specifically remember feeling a close and wonderful affinity with God; I felt as if I had a direct connection to Him and this of course filled me full of joy and happiness.

At the same time, I remember I was disappointed by the teaching in the Sunday School. I recall that this consisted of reading well-known stories from various parts of the Bible, followed by brief, simplistic interpretations – or, sometimes, no interpretation at all. I found this very frustrating because I wanted so much to deepen my knowledge of the Bible. I accept that my desires at that time may have been rather too advanced for most of the young people who attended Sunday School with me but I also had reason to suspect that those who led us at that time were far from knowledgeable about the Bible or Christianity in general. In maturity, I realise that teaching Christianity to young people is never going to be easy; however, I do think that the teacher's Christian knowledge should always be more than sufficient to meet all the needs of their classes, otherwise disappointment and even disengagement may occur.

The Sunday School teaching situation did improve for me when, at a slightly older age, I attended the Young People's Fellowship under the leadership of one of the Local Preachers in the Church. I enjoyed these meetings very much and greatly admired the Preacher for his incisive knowledge of the Bible and the Christian interpretations that he was able to set out for us. The discussions in the Fellowship were very useful in extending my Christian knowledge and belief. However, I must add a cautionary tale from this period.

On one occasion, the Young People's Fellowship biblical study had been about the temptation of Jesus in the wilderness for forty days and forty nights, the well-known story that follows the inspirational biblical account of the baptism of Jesus in the River Jordan. These important accounts appear in all three synoptic Gospels – Matthew, Mark and Luke. At the end of the study, I approached our Fellowship Leader to ask a specific question that was puzzling me.

My question was simple: 'How did the Gospel writers and interpreters of the Temptation story *know* that Jesus spent 40 days and 40 nights in the wilderness?' (This period of time had been emphasised considerably during the study discussion.)

The Leader was silent for a time as he looked at me gravely; then he replied:

'The answer to that question will be revealed to you in good time.'

I was astonished by this answer; in fact I recognised it immediately as no answer at all. I had asked my Christian teacher (whom I respected greatly) what I thought was a simple Christian question – and he had *not answered it!* Furthermore, I thought his response totally inappropriate and I was very disappointed and dispirited as a result. Of course, I realise my reaction then was driven by the intensity of my recently-found faith and by my almost desperate attempts to understand as much as I possibly could about the wonders of my Christian belief.

To the above story, I feel I should add yet another cautionary tale – this time, not based on theological interpretation. This particular event happened to me when I was fifteen and I remember it vividly. One day, when I was at home, the Minister of the Stockland Green Church called in person to see me.

'John, I want to speak to you about membership.' I remember these were his first words. He went on to say that it was clear that I was ready for membership of the Church and that I would attend the forthcoming membership classes he was starting shortly. I disagreed. At that time I felt strongly that I was NOT ready for membership. At that time, I did not want to become a member of the Stockland Green Methodist Church. I did NOT feel ready for what I then regarded as that very important responsibility. Although I recognised that there would certainly be a time in the future when I felt ready, I was convinced that this was NOT the time for such action. I explained all this very carefully and precisely to the Minister.

He brushed aside my view, saying that he was absolutely sure I was ready for membership, so he had already included my name on the list of people who would attend his membership classes. He then provided me with a list of the dates and times of the classes. Finally, he left, saying firmly that he looked forward to seeing me on the first of the class dates.

I did attend the membership classes and I did become a member of the Stockland Green Methodist Church when the sessions were complete. I felt that the Minister had left me no option. But, at that time, I know that I did NOT "feel ready" and, to this day, I feel that it was totally wrong to compel me to do something that was undoubtedly a voluntary matter that involved a personal conviction and nothing else. I am convinced that it is inappropriate to exert pressure of this type upon a young, developing person. Furthermore, I think that the introduction of coercion of this type has the effect of devaluing the intention and reality of the result.

On the other hand, I cannot leave this section about joining the Church without mentioning that a wonderfully attractive girl also attended these same membership classes. She did not usually attend the church at Stockland Green but went to a smaller one at the nearby suburb of Witton; this church was nearer to her home. The Minister at Stockland Green was also assigned to oversee Witton; so prospective members attached to that church would attend membership classes at the larger church.

I knew that this girl's name was Maureen Harris and that she was two years younger than I. It is likely that we exchanged a few brief words occasionally but that was certainly the limit of our contact. I was aware that her parents were important people in the Church. The family was highly musical; her father was the Church Choirmaster at Witton and her mother the Organist. I can best describe

Maureen as the sort of girl that "ordinary" people would admire greatly from afar, knowing for certain that they cannot possibly have ambition for any more than a casual acquaintanceship with such an attractive person. I certainly considered that Maureen was completely out of my reach!

At the age of sixteen, I remember attending the Wesley Guild, another study and fellowship group that met on Wednesday evenings at my Church. One evening, after a session that had included a discussion about the ministry of Local Preachers, a wonderful thing happened. My very good (and very strong!) friend Bob stood up at the meeting to announce decisively that he intended to become a Local Preacher in the Methodist Church; he had been called by God to this work, he said firmly. Everyone was delighted and I recall being extremely proud of my dear friend.

I can report that Bob achieved his ambition by the age of twenty, after being accepted as a candidate for this position by the Methodist Church and following the necessary and testing years of study, examinations and experience. As with everyone who is called by God to this office, I knew that this was a very challenging thing for Bob to do, but I had no doubt that he would succeed. Today, I am delighted to report that Bob continues his calling as a Local Preacher in the Methodist Church.

God be praised!

Meanwhile, home and school life continued with all their tensions and turbulence. I have mentioned earlier how my father was very commercially-orientated from a very early age. I was able to tap into that skill and experience when I decided, at the age of thirteen or so, that I would like to own a bicycle so that I could travel around rather more speedily. At a second-hand bicycle shop not far from my house, I had spotted something suitable, a well-used bicycle that I thought would be fine for my purposes. I asked my father if he would come with me to inspect this bicycle and buy it if it was in good enough condition. I recognised that I was no expert on bicycles! He agreed and, subsequently, we walked along to the shop and entered to inspect the bicycle.

The shopkeeper displayed it for us, pointing out all its features and emphasising its good condition. I thought it looked wonderful but I noticed that my father inspected it with a rather jaundiced eye! At last he addressed the shopkeeper. 'How much is it?' he said in an unenthusiastic tone.

'Five pounds ten shillings,' was the reply. (£5.50, equivalent to around £45 today after inflation)

My father was silent for a few moments. 'I tell you what,' he said, 'I'll give you five pounds for it.'

'Sorry, no,' the shopkeeper replied immediately, 'the price is five pounds ten shillings, I'm afraid.'

Ignoring the shopkeeper totally, my father turned to me. 'Come on,' he said, 'let's go home. We're finished here.' Without pause, he led me outside the shop and was about to start walking home when the shopkeeper appeared behind us. My father glanced at him and, silently, the man held up a hand with five fingers extended. Without a word, my father handed him a five pound note and we left triumphantly, wheeling the bicycle between us.

And, yes, I did learn something about commerce from my father that day!

By this time, my brother Gerald and I had graduated from Junior School to Grammar School and, of course, we found that we had entered a completely new (and alien!) environment. Unlike Junior School, we were now split up and placed in different classes; this seemed to be the policy for dealing with twins. Almost immediately, I recognised that Grammar School was a place where the phrase "survival of the fittest" applied. It was immediately clear to me that the playground was a sort of battle arena, where those who were strong and powerful dominated by violence of varying degrees. If you were not strong and aggressive, as many were not, you kept your head down and tried to survive your schooldays as quietly as possible. If this proved to be impossible, you could seek the shelter of a "gang" and, hopefully, manage to become accepted as a minor member, very much at the beck and call of the "Leader".

I, however, was not weak in either mind or body and my mind-set was far from submissive. I was an experienced battler who did not shirk from confrontations with those who were in more powerful positions than I. It will be recalled also that I felt I had been filled with the power of God. I accept that my experience of God's power at that stage of my life was not the compassion and righteousness of the Christian God I came to know later but rather the powerful and vengeful God found so frequently in the Old Testament of the Bible! I had to become much more mature before I realised the error of my ways and turned positively to Jesus Christ.

So, at Grammar School, I quickly forged a reputation as a "tough guy" who, with increasing frequency, won his playground battles. In due course, other weaker pupils sought my company for protection and became my "gang" members. It was, of course, my ambition to be "Top Man" in the playground. To do this, I needed to challenge the current Top Man, an immensely strong and ferocious character who had held that position for some time. This boy was universally feared by all the pupils and no-one dared to challenge his lofty despotic position – until I came along, that is! In the traditional fashion of such conflict, I challenged this violent, powerful brute to a fight and, after an epic and extremely vicious bout of the most violent and injurious no-holds-barred wrestling, was able to throw him to the ground and pin him there, helpless and squirming. Thus, at a stroke, I became the "Top Man" in the playground, feared and respected by all and I held this position for the rest of my time at the school.

Unfortunately, such dominance in the playground does not translate to power or competence in the classroom. It is in the classroom that you prepare yourself to acquire the educational qualifications that are encouraged by Grammar Schools. I had arrived at the school with a talent for mathematics that had been discovered and honed at my previous school. This talent had been maintained at Grammar School. While I was generally less talented in other subjects, I was nevertheless well-regarded by my various teachers and was expected to do well at GCE "O-levels" – the standard examination of those days. In the Third Form and fast approaching the GCE "O-level" Examinations, I was placed top of the class in mathematics.

I sat a total of seven GCE "O-levels" at examination time and waited for the result with confident serenity. I thought I had probably done well enough to pass all my subjects; this was what my teachers appeared to think. However, when I reflected upon my performance during the examinations, I accepted that my memory had probably failed me at times and I knew that the speed of my writing had been rather slow. None of these thoughts dented my general optimism, however.

In my early teenage years, I had given little thought to my "future". Basically, I suppose I expected to continue in the family business. When Gerald and I left school at the end of the Third Form, we had already been "employed" in the family business for several years, where there was a considerable amount of heavy work to be done (without pay or thanks, as I have mentioned earlier!) We were both fit and strong teenagers, well able to carry out the heavy tasks that our father ordered us to do. I can confirm that large bags of potatoes and boxes of vegetables, etc., are very heavy!

When we had become sufficiently tall, a notable development in our lives concerned the driving of motor vehicles. At this stage, there were several vans in the business and it became our task to turn these vehicles around at the end of the working day, so that they would be ready to leave the yard in the morning. After much trial and error, we became skilled at manoeuvring these vehicles in the very confined space available. Our manoeuvrings were more "fifteen-point turn" than the traditional "three-point turn" of the Driving Test! As all drivers know, controlling a vehicle in a tight space requires delicate skills involving the sophisticated control of clutch, gears, brakes and steering. We had both mastered this skill by our mid-teens; it would stand us in good stead when we were old enough to acquire driving licences.

Unfortunately, where motor vehicles are concerned, accidents can happen – and a particularly unfortunate accident left my father with a broken leg! At this time, one of the vans was kept in a garage. It was a tight fit for the vehicle and my father was directing operations in front of it to ensure that it was parked in the correct spot. On that occasion, my brother Gerald was the unfortunate driver! All was carried out perfectly and my father, finally standing in the very small space between the back wall of the garage and the front of the van, indicated that all was fine and that the vehicle should be shut down. Unfortunately, the clutch was released with the vehicle still in gear and the engine running; it lurched forward, striking my father's legs and knocking him to the floor.

I was with my mother in the house when a very distraught Gerald appeared, saying that he thought he had killed his father! In the ensuing commotion it was soon established that my father had not been killed but it was clear that one leg had been badly injured by the front bumper of the van. An ambulance was called and my father was taken away to hospital. Many hours later, he reappeared back home with a leg dramatically immobilised in plaster from ankle to hip.

Of course, the injury of my father had serious implications for the family business, since he was the driver of the main vehicle. Into the breach stepped my mother! I do not know whether my father suggested (persuaded, cajoled, demanded?) that my mother should learn to drive or whether it was her own idea but, however it was decided, my mother soon obtained a Provisional Driving Licence and started driving the van which I recall was an old Volkswagen "Transporter". Of course, she drove as a learner with "L" plates front and back and my father as her driving instructor, a somewhat explosive situation, I would think! In addition, during the extended period that my father's leg was in plaster, it was necessary to have his rigidly-plastered leg projecting out the nearside window of the van. The whole scenario must have been an arresting sight for other road users!

I think it fair to say that husband/wife driving instruction is not always a success. In fact, I believe it may often be rather less than successful and cause serious conflict in the marriage! So it was with my father and mother – and this was amply demonstrated on one occasion. Although it was never revealed to me what precisely had happened, I know that my mother was driving the van in the middle of the busy city of Birmingham when there was a serious disagreement or altercation of some kind in the van. My mother was a fiery-tempered person who could react rather extremely when provoked. Evidently, my father (with plastered leg projecting from the nearside open window) had said something to cause offence when the van was in the very busiest central part of the city. In response, my mother slammed on the brakes and stopped the vehicle, climbed out, walked off without a backward glance and caught a bus home! To this day, I have no idea how my father was able to cope with this astonishing situation!

Subsequently, my mother went on to pass her Driving Test successfully and left her work in the family shop to sell a whole range of "fancy goods" from her own van. The shop continued on as a family business, managed by a neighbour who had assisted my mother previously.

For Gerald and me, time continued to pass and the work in the family business never slackened. However, we were more than delighted when, at around age sixteen, our father's dictatorial attitude towards us changed dramatically. Like most sudden changes, this was precipitated by a specific and unusual event – in this case, an unexpected physical contact between me and my father. My years of heavy work in the family business had turned me into a powerful, almost fully-grown adult. My father and I now stood eye-to-eye.

On this occasion, I was lifting heavy bags in the store and my father was present. I cannot remember specifically what was happening or what conversation was taking place (if any) but I know that I suddenly grasped him under his arms, lifted him clear of the floor and held him suspended for a time. Clearly, he was totally taken aback by this but said nothing. Although at the time, I had no inkling of the importance of this simple event, it changed everything for Gerald and me. From that time onward, our father's attitude towards us altered completely! He obviously recognised that his sons were now stronger than he and, from that moment on, he treated us with respect. Needless to say, we were delighted. Although we still had to work hard for no financial reward, it was no longer carried out under such unpleasant conditions.

Approaching seventeen, we both applied for Provisional Driving Licences; these were delivered to each of us shortly after our birthday. We were very fortunate that a neighbour then gave us driving lessons in his own car. He proved to be an excellent teacher, always emphasising that smooth control of a vehicle is the essence of good driving. Gerald and I followed his instructions carefully and were very grateful for the time and effort he put into us to make us good drivers. Finally, we took a few professional driving lessons from a local driving school (just to make sure) and, subsequently, we both passed our Driving Tests first time. Our many teenage van manoeuvres, plus our neighbour's excellent teaching augmented by the final polish by the driving school, paid off handsomely for us! Now we were knights of the road, ready for anything!

However, by that time, things had changed radically for me...

5

Adulthood Beckons

After I left school, I have already said that my unfocussed expectation was to continue in the family business. This, however, was certainly not to be. One day, my mother sought my attention and spoke to me about my future: 'John,' she said, 'Gerald is going to work with your father in the family business and you are going to get a job.'

I demurred. 'No, no, it's OK,' I said, laconically, 'I'll just stay here and help them both out, just like I do now.' At that moment, that seemed to be the sensible and comfortable way forward and I thought my mother would capitulate.

I was wrong! My mother was adamant. 'No, John, you will go and get a job. It has been decided.' There was no alternative, it seemed. The matter must have been discussed with my father and a firm decision made.

Days later, my father informed me that he had arranged for us to see the Manager of the local Lloyd's Bank, where he kept his accounts. In those days (unlike now), banking was very much a local affair and there was always a personal relationship between the client and his bank manager, especially if the client was in business. My father told me that the Manager would interview me with a view to a job, probably as a Bank Clerk. This would be a suitable job for me, he thought.

I actually remember being rather excited by this prospect. I thought that a bank would be a good fit for my mathematical talents. Banks, after all, are all about money, aren't they? And money is all about mathematics, isn't it? It seemed to me that a job in a bank would suit me very well. I smiled as I imagined myself as a Bank Manager – and I had little doubt that I would be suitable for that position! 'All in good time,' I thought, with a little inward smile.

On the appointed day, I dressed in my best and we duly arrived at the Bank. The Manager interviewed me with my father present. I can remember very little about this event but I recall that my father did most of the talking, stressing that I had sat seven "O-Levels" at school and mentioning my talent for mathematics. I confirmed that I had come top in mathematics in the Third Form of my Grammar School. However, we advised the Manager that the results of my "O-Levels" were not yet available. I think the Bank Manager was quite impressed but after some thought he turned to my father.

'Mr Nodding,' he said, 'If the boy is good at mathematics, he doesn't want to work in a bank. Why don't you take him to your accountant and get him a job there? Then he can train to become a professional accountant.' I think I perked up at little at this. It sounded interesting. An "accountant" sounded like a very important job and – yes – filled with mathematics! Shortly after this, the interview with the Bank Manager was terminated. Characteristically, my father made no comment as we returned home.

Within a week, it seems that my father had accepted the Bank Manager's recommendation, because he now arranged for us to visit John Lewis & Co., the small accountancy firm in central Birmingham that processed his business accounts. At the interview there, my father's personal accountant, Mr. Benjamin Walker, seated us in his office and explained how young people may be trained in accountancy by working in an accountancy firm.

He told us that qualified accountants like himself could accept suitable trainees as "Articled Clerks". This was an arrangement for a fixed training period of five years, after which the clerks would become Chartered Accountants, provided that they had passed all the examinations required by the Institute of Chartered Accountants. Many accountants, he went on to say, did not pay their Articled Clerks any wage – indeed, the trainees were usually required to pay a fee for the privilege of their training – but he would require no payment to accept me as a clerk "articled" to him and, in addition, he would pay me a wage during the five year training period. The wage was stated to be four pounds (£4.00) per week. At that time, I assumed that this generous offer was made because Mr. Walker was my father's personal accountant.

Mr. Walker then enquired about my GCE "O-level" results (still not available) and said that his offer was conditional upon me having passed a total of six "O-levels". This was a requirement of the Institute, he said. He noted that I had sat seven subjects and looked forward to hearing the outcome. I was delighted with the prospect of working in an accountancy firm and learning from Mr. Walker. I felt confident that I would meet all the requirements of the job. I was more than keen to start working and, to my delight, it was agreed that I could start right away.

So it was that I became a proud and enthusiastic employee of John Lewis & Co., Chartered Accountants. Every weekday, after a bus journey from my home to central Birmingham, I arrived joyfully at 9 a.m. and climbed the front steps that led to the firm's suite of rooms. The Senior Partner, Mr. John Lewis, occupied a large room at the front of the property and Mr. Walker had a separate office towards the rear. The other rooms included a large General Office where the remainder of the staff worked. There were two Senior Clerks (both men around fifty years of age) and several other clerks and typists. It was a busy and purposeful establishment, full of activity.

Having arrived, I worked diligently until 5.30 p.m. with a one hour lunch break from 1 to 2 p.m., when I ate a modest and inexpensive lunch (I recall it was invariably an "Egg Brunch" in the restaurant of Gray's, a nearby department store). At that time, I suppose my formal status was "Provisional Articled Clerk" but the reality of my job was the office junior! As the newest and youngest person there, all the lowest-level tasks were handed to me!

I remember that every day I had to make everything neat and tidy in the offices, wind the clock, renew the desk blotting paper and fill the inkwells (yes, they were using liquid ink and dipping pens!). Of course, I was responsible for making the tea and coffee which was done in an extremely filthy, cramped kitchen. Also, I was the office filing clerk. The accountants had a unique way of dealing with the client files that they had worked upon; they threw them haphazardly on the floor! I had to retrieve the bulky folders, neaten them up and replace them back in the filing cabinets in their correct places. Furthermore, when time permitted, I started to clean the disgraceful kitchen and eventually imposed some degree of hygiene there, to the grateful admiration of all.

After I acquired my Driving Licence, a rather more pleasurable duty involved re-parking Mr Walker's very smart car in an appropriate parking space near the office. Routinely, he was unable to find a suitable parking place when he arrived in the morning and had to park some distance away. He would then hand me the keys to the car with instructions to find a parking space close to the office.

Everything went swimmingly for six weeks or so – I was on "Cloud Nine!" *And then it happened.* I returned home to find that the results of the GCE "O-level" examinations had arrived. I remember sitting and staring at these with absolute disbelief. I had passed in only two subjects!

Mathematics (of course) and Geography. I had failed the other five. Surely this was a mistake? But, no, the longer I sat there, the more I knew that it was the truth. I was absolutely devastated by this turn of events. Blackness descended. What would happen now? My mind blanked. I couldn't think, I was so shocked. Then, after timeless minutes (was it hours?), a new and terrible thought occurred to me. If I could not become an Articled Clerk to Mr. Walker (and I now knew this to be a certainty), did this mean that I would be dismissed from the firm? After all, it was an Articled Clerk they wanted, wasn't it? Not an office junior or an office boy!

So it was that a haggard, distraught figure arrived at John Lewis & Co. the following day. In due course, I crept in to see Mr. Walker and forced myself to communicate the terrible news. Time passed, I do not know how long. Mr. Walker spoke and eventually I understood that he wanted me to stay at the firm, not of course as an Articled Clerk but as the office junior; everyone had been very pleased with my work, he said. However, he would need to reduce my pay from four pounds to three pounds ten shillings (£3.50) per week. He went on to propose that I should study for my missing "O-levels" at evening classes. I should also plan to take the Institute's entry examination at the end of the year. He confirmed that a total of six GCE "O-levels" **or** a pass in the Institute's entry examination would make it possible for me to become his Articled Clerk. Until then, I would be the office junior.

I recognised a lifeline, indeed, an offer I could not refuse. I accepted gratefully and decided I had to "give it my all". So began a year of absolutely frenetic activity for me. I continued to work hard and diligently at the firm. Then, four evenings a week (Monday to Thursday), I attended evening classes at a college near my home, studying for four of the subjects I had failed. Friday evening was also a study time; that was when I tackled my homework. In addition, during the year I prepared for the Institute's examination.

Eventually, I completed my herculean efforts at the evening classes and sat the four GCE "O-level" examinations. To sit the Institute's examination, I had to travel to London, where I stayed very inexpensively at the YMCA Hostel, in a bleak and scrupulously clean room. At last, the days arrived when the results of my examinations were published. I had passed three of my four GCE "O-levels"; this was, of course, insufficient for my purposes. However, to my great joy, I found that I had passed the Institute's examination and so was at last eligible to become an Articled Clerk to Mr Walker. By dint of considerable and sustained effort, I had finally succeeded in reversing the ill-fortune of my schooldays!

At John Lewis & Co. I was subsequently upgraded to the dizzy heights of Articled Clerk and my weekly wage shot up (!) from three pounds ten shillings to a heady four pounds per week. Of course, I was still the office junior as well and still had to carry out all the chores that I did before! However, now that I had become an Articled Clerk, Mr Walker and the Senior Clerks began to teaching me tasks in accountancy and I was also allowed to leave the office for external audits. I applied myself diligently and learned a great deal about accounting work in the following year.

Meanwhile, over this extended period of time between leaving school and becoming an Articled Clerk, a great deal else had happened to me. For one thing, I had grown up (to some degree, at least!). During the whole period, however, the Church remained an important and positive influence in my life and it was from church sources that most of my friends came.

When I was eighteen years old, our Church acquired a new minister. (In the Methodist Church, ministers move from church to church throughout their careers, usually after five years at each.) The new minister, Rev. Stanley Johnson, was one of the most powerful, charismatic and energetic people I have ever known. He had a great influence on me and I know he was very highly regarded by many other people in our Church. I certainly admired him immensely and listened with great care to everything that he said.

It was around this time that I asked my father if I could accompany him to a prayer meeting which met at the Church every Thursday at the very early hour of 7.00 am. (i.e. before the start of daily work.) This was a meeting that my father attended invariably, driving there in his car and returning in time to open up his business in George Road. I am afraid I do not know whether my father was pleased that I should want to attend the prayer meeting; when I asked to accompany him, he agreed to take me any time I wanted to go but I have no recollection of any further comment. As far as I can recall, the journeys there and back were completed largely in silence.

Looking back, it must have taken a lot of courage for me to attend this meeting but, of course, I did have the Spirit of the Lord burning within me! During the first few weeks I attended the prayer meeting, I did not speak out my prayers but merely participated in silence; I was still too diffident to pray out loud in such serious Christian company! However, after a few weeks, the Minister (who always led the prayer meeting) approached me and suggested I might like to start my spoken contributions by reading aloud one or more verses of a hymn; he reminded me that all hymns were prayers and therefore were most suitable for that purpose. I was very happy to accept his suggestion. I cannot remember what hymn I chose but this excellent advice soon led me to speak out my own prayers *extempore* (spoken without preparation). Soon I was praying fluently at the meeting – perhaps the experiences of my Scout Camp storytelling also helped to give me confidence!

I have already mentioned that Rev. Stanley Johnson was an extremely dedicated man who directed his energies to all parts of the Church. He was, of course, very interested in the youth who attended his churches (Stockland Green and Witton) and had meetings at the manse called "Squashes", to which many young people came. The meetings were very popular and the name "Squash" accurately describes what they were like! We all sang lustily and Stanley also used these meetings to discuss many aspects of Christian life. We had many stimulating conversations. However, one surprising thing I do remember. While Stanley was generally tolerant in his views, this most certainly did not extend to alcoholic drink! Alcoholic drink, he said, was the work of the Devil. Drinking it was a SIN! Of course all the young people agreed fervently!

At this time, the father of a friend of mine in the Church routinely invited a group of his son's Christian friends to come to his house after the Sunday morning service. Half a dozen or so (including me) usually attended. My friend's father never attended the Church but he seemed to enjoy the company of the friends that his son brought each week. On just one occasion (I don't know why), the man said he wanted to offer us all a sherry to drink (alcohol – the demon drink!). Although his son immediately shouted "No", the man produced a bottle of sherry and a tray of glasses and began asking around the circle of my friends. As he worked around, everyone said "No" very firmly. They all had been taught about SIN by Stanley Johnson!

As each person curtly declined, I began to feel very uncomfortable. I felt strongly that everyone was being extremely impolite and I became increasingly embarrassed. This pleasant and generous man was offering us his hospitality and all my friends were refusing brusquely. So, despite the admonitions of Stanley Johnson ringing in my ears, when the man came to me, I said "Yes, thank you, I will join you" and a small glass of sherry was poured for me. Finally, he poured his own and he and I sipped our sherries to the shocked disapproval of the assembled company!

While I admired our minister greatly, I have never been in favour of imposing extremist views on others, especially if these have the potential to harm. Had I not said "Yes" on this occasion, I believe our kindly host would have been embarrassed that his hospitality and generosity had been tersely refused by everyone. I could not allow this to happen.

However, I think this is probably the only time that I rejected Stanley Johnson's teaching and advice. I recall one piece of advice he gave me that literally changed my life – and changed it in a most wonderful way. I will always be most grateful to him for this. This is what happened…

I had been to one of the enjoyable "Squashes". It seems that I was the last to leave the manse that evening – perhaps Stanley had asked me to wait; maybe he had told me he had something important to say to me. In any case, I vividly remember us both standing on the front steps of the manse. The words he spoke to me are forever emblazoned on my heart!

'John,' he said quietly, 'I think you should go after that Maureen Harris.'

I looked at him with some astonishment. *"Go after Maureen Harris?"* The words reverberated inside my skull in a tattoo of disbelief. I have no idea what I replied and the next memory I have is walking away down the road, my head in a whirl.

Maureen Harris, you will recall, was the beautiful, wonderful, clever, unattainable girl who had been at the membership classes with me. Now when I say "with me", of course I don't mean that! She had not been "with me" in any way – far from it! She had merely been present in the room as we took the membership classes. However, it is true that I knew a little about her life, because, although Maureen normally attended the smaller Witton Church with her best friend Cheryl (and so I did not see her routinely), I did receive information about her from my girlfriend of the time – Cheryl!

Obviously, Stanley's recommendation to me made me consider the possibility of a friendship with Maureen. Was it possible? Would she be willing to have anything to do with me? I didn't know but, with Stanley's words ringing in my ears, I determined to try. Firstly, I thought, I need to improve myself – make myself more attractive. One important way to do that, I decided, was to learn to dance properly. In those days, dancing together was a primary way to "get close" to a partner. 'That's it!' I thought, 'I'll become a decent dancer!'

So I went to a series of dancing classes where I was taught a number of the dances that were popular at the time. As a much improved dancer, I now felt more confident in my ability to impress my partner on the dance floor and hoped that I might have the opportunity to dance with Maureen in due course. You may imagine that this was never far from my mind!

I think I was around twenty years old when a group of my friends and I decided to have a night out at a premier ballroom in central Birmingham. In those days, dance halls were big business and many of these were located in former cinemas that had declined as the influence of television strengthened. The new dance halls were lavishly fitted out with spacious dance floors, a range of bars and cafés and top quality big band music. In short, for the young men and women of the day, they were the "places to be"; very much the places where romance blossomed. We were a group of ten young men and ladies who attended the ballroom that night.

I went with Cheryl, my girlfriend; *but I came home with Maureen!*

6

Maureen

The next few years of my life were truly amazing! In so many ways, I found it almost impossible to believe it. *Maureen Harris had become MY girlfriend!* These were the words, dazzling and iridescent, that constantly spun around in the projection of my mind. How could this goddess, this most beautiful and wonderful person, this extremely talented and clever young lady, this most gentle, loving and spiritual of creatures ... be MY girlfriend? Yet I knew it to be true. The proof was there in her presence. Incredibly, she wanted to be with me – and no-one else!

Of course there were many other suitors; numerous other hopefuls! This is bound to happen with girls like Maureen. There were many young men, mostly associated with the Church, who cast distinctly covetous and admiring eyes on her; young men who made tentative (or sometimes not so tentative!) advances to her. However, she rejected them all. I particularly remember one young man, a fine, good looking young fellow, made even more attractive by the fact that he possessed the ultimate in machismo – a swashbuckling, impressive motorcycle! I recall that he tried very hard with Maureen, even to the extent of "arranging" for his motorcycle to break down right in front of her house. Of course, he then had to knock at the door to seek help! ... all to no avail, I am happy to say. Maureen continued to reject all advances, including his, in favour of me. To my delight, she told me she didn't want anything to do with any of these others.

Now we had a routine. We met two or three times a week, on weekday evenings and for longer periods on Saturdays. Wherever we went or whatever we did, I was always under instructions to return Maureen back to her home by ten thirty in the evening. Actually, this was quite a convenient time for me, since the last bus to my home area departed from near her house at five past eleven. If I missed that, I would need to walk – and it was quite a long way! So, between ten-thirty and eleven o'clock, there was sufficient time for a cup of tea and a slice of cake.

The scene was always played like this: When we arrived at her home, Maureen disappeared into the kitchen with her mother to prepare the tea, while I conversed with her father, Norman Harris. I suppose this might have been a trial for many young men but I found Maureen's father a most delightful man and was able to chat easily with him. In fact, as time went on, I began to feel extremely comfortable in Maureen's house, which was filled with a wonderful ambiance of respect, goodness and love. I increasingly found that I was much more comfortable in the Harris' home than in my own and I looked forward eagerly to my visits to that house.

Of course the Church continued to be a significant focus for both Maureen and me and some of our evenings together were at the young people's Squash meetings at the manse. It was at such a meeting that the Minister proposed the formation of visiting pairs who would befriend elderly people who were lonely and largely ignored. As a man of action, he immediately called for volunteers and, when many offered themselves for this ministry, he formed us into our pairs. Initially, I was paired with a young man who was a friend of mine but, when he dropped out after a while, I sought permission to replace him with Maureen. I was delighted when this was agreed. Now we were officially a "visiting pair" and we spent many enjoyable evenings with elderly ladies and gentlemen, forming significant and meaningful bonds of friendship with them.

In the same spirit, around Christmas time, we visited very poor families in the area and took toys along to give to their children, who would otherwise have received nothing on Christmas Day. On one occasion, we arrived at a very shabby and barren house where we were astounded to find that there were no chairs to sit upon! I remembered that the Witton Church had some spare chairs stacked in a storage area and Maureen and I decided we would provide this very poor family with chairs from this source. Maureen's father was contacted and quickly agreed to provide his car as necessary transport so we were able to deliver the chairs very quickly. We were very happy that this unfortunate family would at least be able to sit down for Christmas! During all the time we were serving as a visiting pair, Maureen and I were happy to be able to serve God and the community in this way.

I was extremely impressed that all the members of the Harris family were such talented musicians. Maureen was a gifted pianist and her brother David played the trombone. In addition, Maureen had a remarkable singing voice with an exceptionally wide range. From a young age, she could sing with ease opera parts that were pitched for either contralto or soprano. Her voice was heard many times in performance when she was a student at the prestigious Birmingham School of Music. Furthermore, she was offered a scholarship opportunity to study at a USA College of Music but decided against leaving the family (and me!). Of course I was greatly relieved since I would have been devastated to be apart from her.

Maureen had been my serious (*very* serious!) girlfriend for about a year when another love came into my life.

My first car! Like all young men with driving licences, it was of course my ambition to own my own car and it was Maureen who provided me with an unique opportunity to achieve this.

At this time, she was working as a secretary at Colliers, a large car dealership in the centre of Birmingham. Maureen was aware of my ambition and obviously kept her eyes open for any bargains that might be suitable for my (our!) purposes. It may well be that she confided in the salesman and asked them to alert her to anything that might be available in a (very) modest price range.

One day, she told me that she had spotted a possibility – a Ford Prefect saloon that had obviously been a part-exchange for a new car from the dealership. Not knowing a great deal about Ford Prefects, I asked her to tell me what it was like. Well, she said, it was sort of beige in colour and looked quite nice, as far as she could see. I was aware that Ford had used the name "Prefect" for models over a considerable period of time, so I knew this car could be anything from "quite old" to "relatively new".

'Do you know how old it is?' I asked.

'No,' she replied 'but it certainly isn't new! I think it looks in decent enough condition, though.'

'How much do Colliers want for it?' I asked.

'Well,' she said, 'they weren't sure, but I negotiated with the Sales Manager. In the end he said you could have it for ten·pounds!'

My mouth dropped open. 'Ten pounds,' I repeated in a whisper.

She smiled at my astonishment. 'Yes. I negotiated with him. Hard!'

'Wow! I'd better come and see it as soon as possible!'

Subsequently, we inspected the Ford Prefect, the ten pound car! I cannot remember its year of manufacture but it may have been around fifteen years old and had obviously been driven many miles. Nevertheless, it seemed to be sound enough, as far as I could tell. Anyway, there's a limit to what you can expect for ten pounds!

So, due to Maureen's cleverness and persistence, I bought the beautiful, beige Ford Prefect from Colliers for ten pounds. A year's insurance cost more than the car (£14, Third Party, Fire and Theft – of course I couldn't afford Comprehensive!) and, in due course, I triumphantly drove the car away from Colliers. Surely everyone can remember that day when they picked up their very first car and drove it away as "King of the Road"! I drove the Prefect many miles during the following years. It proved to be only moderately reliable and there were periodic breakdowns. As the impecunious owner of such a car, you needed to become very resourceful!

I recall Maureen and myself making a rather brave and epic journey to visit an aunt of hers who lived about 90 miles away. On the journey, no doubt because of the increased speed I was imposing on my elderly car, I noted with regret that steam was curling up from under the bonnet and knew we were about to break down. This had happened before and I knew it was likely to be due to the failure of one of the rubber radiator hoses that circulates the cooling water from the radiator and through the engine. So we stopped and I opened the bonnet to clouds of steam. Sure enough, there was a split in the radiator hose and much of the water that cooled the engine had been lost. With the unconcern of the young, I was unperturbed by this. I knew what must be done.

First, the radiator cap had to be removed to release the steam pressure in the system. I knew this was a very dangerous manoeuvre that can cause serious injury. However, using an old thick cloth (no doubt carried for precisely this purpose), I was able to seize the extremely hot radiator cap and remove it without serious injury, by leaping back nimbly as soon as the lethal jet of steam blasted out! When the steam finally stopped billowing out and some degree of calm had been restored, Maureen asked me how we were going to fix the problem.

'Well,' I replied, 'we need to repair this rubber hose and then refill the system with water once the engine has cooled down.'

'How do we repair the hose,' she asked doubtfully, 'that looks like a very big split in it.'

'Don't worry, I can repair it,' I said with supreme confidence, 'but I need your help.'

'Fine,' she said, 'What do you need me to do?'

'I can repair it if you give me one of your nylon stockings!' I replied. 'If I tie it tightly around the damaged area, it will seal the split shut and we'll be able to proceed.' I felt suitably smug as I explained this!

I think she was surprised but she disappeared and returned shortly afterwards to hand me one of her nylons without comment. 'Thanks,' I said, as I wrapped it carefully around the hose and tied it very tightly. We had to wait a while for the engine to cool down but eventually I was able to refill the system from a jerry can of water I carried in the car boot for precisely this purpose. I then replaced the radiator cap and started the engine, watching the "tights repair area" carefully. It held successfully!

I turned to Maureen. 'Looks like we've done it,' I said, embracing her joyfully, 'I really must take you with me everywhere!'

It was in this period of our life that a serious tragedy happened in the Harris family. Maureen's brother David was travelling with a group of friends in a small van when it left the road and hit a tree by the roadside. David was thrown from the van and suffered a severe blow to the head which knocked him unconscious. He was taken to hospital and found to have very severe concussion, which had sent him into a deep coma. The medical staff told us that, in general, the longer a patient lies in a coma, the more severe the injury to the brain; also, the chance of recovery diminishes as the period of the coma lengthens. Lying in an Intensive Care bed, David's coma lasted a full eight weeks, by which time he was not expected to survive. If he did awake from his coma, the medical specialists said, his recovery would be extremely slow and the quality of his life highly impaired.

This was a time of great sadness and distress for the family, who thought that they would lose David, especially as the period of his coma extended. I can remember visiting the hospital a number of times with the family and seeing this totally inert figure on the bed, clearly supported by a range of mechanical devices that constantly maintained and monitored his vital functions. As far as I was concerned, I was looking at a body with little or no life left in it and I did not expect him to survive. As someone who had grafted myself on to the Harris family, David's condition filled me with pity and sorrow.

There was muted joy when, to the surprise of all, David began to regain consciousness after eight full weeks; obviously his journey to consciousness at that time was slow and painful. When he became sufficiently awake and aware, he no longer needed to be in the Intensive Care ward and was transferred to a special ward for men recovering from serious head injuries. I remember visiting this ward and being filled anew with horror and despair; as I cast my gaze around, I saw a dozen or so barely-alive men struggling to achieve the most basic elements of body and mind control – and often failing. I thought of this room as a place of absolute despair and I knew positively that David – and all the others who were there – would never be able to return to any sort of normality; that is, if they did not lose the battle completely and lose their lives. I remember wondering whether the latter option was preferable.

I was wrong. Totally. Although David was in that room for a very long time – certainly more than a year, he did regain control of his mind and body, although progress was agonisingly slow. Eventually, he regained an incredible 95% functionality of mind and body and was able to return to a good quality of normal life. I regard his recovery as a miracle.

Time passed and my relationship with Maureen continued to deepen. By this time, we had been together "seriously" for three years or so and my love for her was becoming more and more powerful. It is no understatement to say that I was totally infatuated with her. Now my thoughts began to turn to marriage because I knew that she was the person with whom I wanted to share the rest of my life. In other words, I started to think about "popping the question"! Although I was confident that Maureen loved me, I was nevertheless rather nervous about proposing marriage. What if she was quite happy with the *status quo*? This was certainly one concern that I had. However, the moment eventually arrived, when we were all alone on a balmy, serene and starry night, when romance was palpably powerful in the air. Knowing this to be a perfect moment, I gathered my courage and asked her to marry me. There was an agonising pause; then she said "yes"!

This was absolutely wonderful but I knew there was yet another stage in the process of betrothal (to use an old-fashioned word!). I understood that it was necessary for me to ask her father for permission to marry his daughter. I am sure that many of the young people of today would scoff at such a step; life seems to be so much more casual now – and so much more selfish, too. Anyway, I was convinced that it was a step I must take. When I thought about it, I found I was distinctly worried about the procedure. What would I say? How would I say it? In what circumstances? I was also worried about the outcome. What if he said "NO"? I knew that Maureen respected her father greatly and would not want to go against his wishes. So this was a matter that occupied my mind a great deal and I began to look for suitable situations to have this most private of conversations with Mr Harris.

Eventually, I spotted the perfect opportunity and decided I must seize the bull by the horns (perhaps an unfortunate figure of speech!). It was the end of a Sunday service at the Witton Church and Mr Harris was the duty Church Steward. I had observed him enter the minister's vestry and knew that he was alone in that room. I knocked at the door and shuffled in nervously. Mr Harris was there and looked at me quizzically. I cannot remember the words I used but, screwing up my courage to the maximum, I asked him for his daughter's hand in marriage! I was more than overjoyed when he reacted with delight, shaking my hand warmly, replying with his permission and congratulating me with great enthusiasm.

Thus, Maureen and I were formally betrothed! With the help of Maureen's mother, who had some advantageous connections with the famous and prestigious Birmingham Jewellery Quarter, a beautiful diamond engagement ring was purchased by me and it was then a great delight to see my wonderful fiancée wearing this ring as a sparkling token of our engagement to each other. The months reeled past so quickly as we spent as much time as possible with each other. Of course there were many discussions about the detail of our forthcoming marriage – where would it be, who would be invited and, last but not least, what would it cost! We determined that it should be a simple wedding, carried out (of course) in the church at Witton. However, because my church at Stockland Green had bigger rooms and more facilities to cater for larger numbers, we decided to ask that the wedding reception should be held there. Over a period, all this was arranged and the wedding was set for early September 1968.

In the midst of all this happiness and excitement, a very sad and sudden event devastated the Harris family. In February 1968, six months before the wedding, Maureen's beloved father, Mr Norman Harris, suffered a massive heart attack while sitting quietly in an armchair in his house. The Emergency Services were called and arrived quickly; however, they were unable to resuscitate him and, in due course, confirmed that he had died. He was only fifty-six years old.

I was working on an external audit when I received a frantic phone call from Maureen. The terrible news shocked me deeply and filled me with overwhelming sadness. It is no overstatement to say that Norman Harris was a man whom I loved and respected greatly; in fact, I have already stated earlier that he had become like a father to me. Thus, my personal grief was more akin to the loss of a much-loved genetic parent. Immediately, I determined that I must support the Harris family as strongly as I could during their time of bereavement.

From a relatively early age, we all know that the life we live contains incidences of death, when people (instinctively, I suppose we think "old people") we have known disappear suddenly from our lives. When we are very young, our parents often shield us from the reality of these deaths, explaining merely that the kindly old relatives we have known have "gone away to be with God", or such similar phrases. Although the truth gradually dawns as we develop, the all-pervading agony of personal bereavement does not arrive until a truly loved one is lost. There is always a first time for this happening; for me, Norman Harris' death was that first time.

In the weeks and months that followed, I did my best to support the Harris family. As a family, we considered whether it would be appropriate to postpone the wedding but it was agreed that Norman Harris would not have wished us to do that. So the September wedding date that had already been arranged was retained.

Maureen and I were married on September 2nd, 1968. It was a blustery, unsettled day. By this time, a new minister had taken over from my wonderful friend, Rev.

Stanley Johnson – who had been personally responsible for "winding me up and setting me off" towards the love of my life, Maureen Harris! The new minister, Rev. Ken Street, was a lovely, sincere young man, very much in the early part of his ministerial career. Before the wedding, I noticed that he was becoming increasingly nervous and tense. Eventually, I went to see him in the vestry and found him in a very highly agitated state. He admitted to me that he had never conducted a marriage before and, as a result, he was extremely worried at the prospect. I sat and talked to him for a while and eventually managed to convince him that all would go well!

In the event, our wedding was simple and beautiful. We were delighted to be married in the intimacy of the Witton Methodist Church by Ken Street, who performed the ceremony perfectly. However, another significant event has to be reported. During the progress of the ceremony, there was a storm and we could hear heavy rain pounding the church roof above our heads. Then, just as we were leading up to the marriage vows, a deafening clap of thunder shook the church.

Maureen leaned towards me and, looking into my eyes, whispered:

'That's my Dad.'

I believe it was.

The reception at my church was a joyful affair attended by family and our many friends. The only thing I can remember about my speech was my grateful thanks to a friend who worked as the caretaker of a nearby Jewish Cemetery. At the reception, he appeared laden with flowers which made an absolutely magnificent display all around the Church Hall. It was a very kind and thoughtful gesture and I did not, of course, enquire too closely about the origin of so many magnificent blooms!

After a delightful honeymoon in Keswick, the new Nodding family settled into a modest house in Witton, with the inevitable minimum of furniture. I remember that this house was bought for the princely sum of £3,250 (Strictly speaking, like most young people, I actually purchased a small piece of the house and the rest was a huge mortgage!). We were, of course, ecstatically happy. We had deliberately chosen a house close to the Harris family home, so that we would be able to support Maureen's mother, suddenly deprived of the support of her beloved husband of many years and the almost simultaneous loss of her daughter by marriage. This was an arrangement that worked well for the following years, as we were able to see her almost daily.

7

A Blessèd Life

At the age of twenty-four, I now entered a blessèd period in my life. At work, I was still toiling towards my goal of becoming a fully-qualified Chartered Accountant and remained unswerving in my determination to succeed. It will be recalled that my Articled Clerkship to Mr Benjamin Walker at John Lewis & Co. would come to an end after a fixed term of five years – I was twenty-two when this happened and can report that, by that time, my initial four pounds per week wage had risen during the years to arrive at a heady eight pounds and ten shillings per week (£8.50)!

As far as Benjamin Walker was concerned, the plan for his Articled Clerk had been to teach me by giving me wide experience of the range of accountancy work that was handled at the firm. The teaching was carried out either by Mr. Walker himself or, sometimes, by one of the Senior Clerks at the firm. This system had worked well and I learned a great deal about the work of an accountant during the five years I was employed there.

In parallel to this training, all other academic and technical aspects of accountancy were to be studied by means of a "correspondence course" (usually called "distance learning" today) that was run by a company called Foulkes Lynch. The course included Institute of Accountancy examinations which, if passed, should lead to the trainee's acceptance by the Institute as a fully-qualified Chartered Accountant. The five year training schedule for Articled Clerks led to a range of interim accountancy examinations after 2½ years. If passes in all the subjects were achieved satisfactorily, a further 2½ years of study preceded the final Institute of Accountancy examinations. Success in these allowed the trainee (at long last!) to be accepted as a qualified Chartered Accountant by the Institute.

Unfortunately, I did not find that this correspondence course method of academic education was successful for me. It seems that this was the experience of many others as well, because I knew that the pass rate for all these examinations was consistently low. I had to re-sit some parts of the interim examinations several times. Then, after the interim hurdles had finally been jumped successfully, I found I was having the same trouble with the range of final examinations until someone recommended me to attend a special short course run privately by a particular chartered accountant in Birmingham. This, I was told, would teach me successful examination techniques – specifically, how to pass the examinations I was struggling with! At considerable personal expense, I enrolled on this course and found it revelatory. Subsequently, when I re-sat the Institute's final accountancy examinations once again, I passed them all with ease. It remains my opinion that the system of study I had to struggle with for all these years was unsatisfactory and inadequate in so many ways. I sincerely hope that this is not the case today.

During all this time of study, however, I learned many practical aspects of accountancy from my employers. My first employer dealt mainly with small businesses (shops, farms, local manufacturers) and this gave me valuable experience at that level. I remember many occasions when

A Small Piece of Pure Gold

I produced (beautiful!) sets of formal accounts from huge unorganised piles of farming records, with many papers showing a centre hole where they had been physically "spiked" as the routine and only system of filing at the farm! It was a significant thrill for me to impose perfect order on such chaos!

When I left Lewis & Co. in 1966, I joined the prominent accountancy firm of Howard Smith Thomson which in due course became the very well-known accountants, Price Waterhouse, during the time I was working there. Here, previous success in all my interim accountancy examinations allowed me to be offered employment as an "ordinary" accountant – and to more than double my salary. Needless to say, I was extremely pleased with this significant elevation in remuneration!

Price Waterhouse (Cooper came later) was a huge organisation with a number of specialist departments within it (e.g. audits, taxation, incomplete records) and I was able to gain specialised experience in these various departments. In addition, some of the external audits I was involved in were carried out in awesome surroundings. For instance, I will never forget visits to the British Gas central office in the Midlands and viewing an absolutely vast and astounding room where no less than 1,400 people worked in small segmented compartments! Price Waterhouse also did accountancy work for Birmingham City Council; this involved visiting the extremely impressive Council House building, still perched magnificently at the top of one of Birmingham's highest hills. It felt like a wonderful privilege to be able to gain access to this fine building.

It was during my time at Price Waterhouse that I married Maureen, so the man who arrived at his desk each day was filled with the energy and good spirits of one deeply in love! Within two years (and with the help of the "examination technique course"), I achieved my long-held ambition of becoming a fully-qualified Chartered

Accountant. Proudly, I added the wonderful initials "ACA" to my name. In 1970, life was truly delightful!

Not long after, I made my next career move by leaving Price Waterhouse and joining a medium-sized accountancy firm in Birmingham. This move would benefit me by extending my experience to all sizes of accountancy firms. In addition, Neville, Russell & Co. employed me as a manager, which elevated my status. My special focus in the firm was to be "systems", which had become a specific interest of mine, as it was concerned with coordination and efficiency within the business span of my profession. In the following decades, the development of computer and electronic data processing facilities changed for ever the meaning of "systems" as defined in 1970; my own interest and expertise kept pace with these developments and my knowledge of computing programming and techniques became a significant advantage for my own career prospects.

Hilton Advertising was a busy advertising agency whose main offices were in Birmingham. My firm was employed as Hilton's accountants and I became their auditor. It was clear to me that they were highly successful in their business, providing very creative initiatives for a list of national retail clients. The firm was led by two directors, a father and son team, Mr Ted Hilton and his son John. There were twenty or so other employees in the offices at Birmingham with others in subsidiary offices elsewhere in England. I was able to establish an excellent relationship with the management of this company, especially with the Senior Director, Mr Ted Hilton.

By the time I had twice audited the Hilton accounts, I had become an expert in their financial structures and procedures, which I judged were not serving them well. In consequence, I sought a discussion with Ted Hilton and suggested that his Agency would benefit greatly from the acquisition of a Financial Director. Subsequently, no doubt after considerable internal discussions, Ted

A Small Piece of Pure Gold

Hilton informed me that my recommendation was to be accepted. To my surprise, he offered the position to me and suggested a very generous salary. I was delighted to accept and became the third Director of the Company. My new position allowed me to buy a 5% stake in the Company, which I was pleased to do.

Obviously, with my focus on "systems" efficiency, I was able to impose much more effective financial structures within the company and, as the years passed, introduced the latest computer and data processing solutions to increase efficiency even further. Of course, commercial computers were virtually non-existent at the beginning of the 1970s but, in the latter part of the decade, a few leading companies began to install some degree of electronic computing into their organisations. I remember visiting the offices of Saatchi & Saatchi in the city of Gloucester after they had installed a very early NCR computer system and gaining some very valuable knowledge of this rudimentary equipment.

Back at Hilton Advertising, I had also noted that the company had considerable cash deposits languishing in low or zero-interest bank accounts. With the permission of the Directors, I invested this money and, within a year, increased its value considerably, earning myself a substantial bonus in the process! Also, over the years, the company continued to expand and I was heavily involved in the establishment of several branch offices across England. In the end, in addition to the main office in Birmingham, there were branch offices in London, Manchester, Hemel Hempstead and Bournemouth.

From the very beginning, I had excellent relations with the Hiltons, especially with the Senior Director, Ted. He was a very fine man, for whom I had great respect. When we travelled together on the train (always Standard Class!) on our frequent visits to the subsidiary offices of the firm, we found that we always had a great deal to discuss, not only on accountancy matters but on all aspects of life in general. Ted Hilton was a very wise man who became like a father figure to me.

In addition, I formed a long-standing friendship with Ted's daughter, Beverley and her husband Tony Ostrin, who lived in Liverpool. Tony was a solicitor who sometimes worked at Hiltons. Our friendship began when Tony and his family came to see me in Sutton Coldfield. This was on a business matter but they were also on their way to a family holiday. When their car broke down some miles from my home, I went to rescue them. With a car that could not be repaired right away, I saw that they were now stranded in Sutton Coldfield, far from the destination of their family holiday. I therefore insisted that Tony should borrow my car so that they could have their holiday on schedule. That week, I travelled on the bus to work! Thereafter, we were very close family friends for many years, visiting each other periodically in our homes. We had many wonderful times together.

Meanwhile, Maureen and I had not forgotten our Christian commitments at home. We attended the Witton Church assiduously and participated in many ways in their Christian aims, with a special focus on the younger people. A significant part of the structure of Methodist Church organisation is the formation of "house fellowships" within each church. The fellowships are registered as part of the church structure and are overseen by the minister. All church attendees are encouraged to attend and belong to a house fellowship. The fellowships meet regularly, usually on a schedule of weekday evenings that are led by a Church member, normally at his or her house. This provides a more intimate form of worship and provides steadfast fellowship, support and strong social cohesion for groups of like-minded Christians, as well as informal Christian teaching in a relaxed setting.

Shortly after Maureen and I settled into our new home in Witton, we established a new house fellowship. For many years, both Maureen and I had been enthusiastic scholars of the Bible and we knew that our circle of young friends in the Church were keen to expand their Christian knowledge. Maureen and I were the joint leaders of this group and the meetings were usually attended by half a dozen or so friends from the Church. When gathered, we shared freely our joys and sorrows in true Christian fellowship. In addition, we studied interpretations of parts of the Bible that were relevant to our Christian seasons, often using the famous William Barclay series of biblical commentaries to inform our discussions and conclusions. At that time, Dr William Barclay was a very well-known British theologian who, in the late 1950s, had written a succession of extremely clear and detailed interpretations of the New Testament books of the Bible, under the title of "The Daily Bible Study" series. These were published inexpensively as sixteen separate small volumes and were very popular at the time; the series is still published today.

The house fellowship met throughout the whole of our six year occupancy of the house in Witton. During that time, we all expanded our Christian knowledge considerably and deepened our powerful bonds of Christian comradeship with each other. The meetings were an especially thrilling time for Maureen and me and we always remembered them with great affection.

Before Maureen and I were married, we discussed having a family. We were both keen to do this and hoped that we could have several children. We both believed that children would be born to us in God's good time; in the event, we were delighted when Maureen became pregnant in the autumn of 1970, just two years after our marriage. In one sense, I look back in amazement at this time. Over the months of pregnancy, while the growing "bump" is a remarkable sight to behold, almost nothing prepares you for the physical movements of a new life that you can feel (and see!) in the later months. This amazing growing life becomes a new and extremely powerful bond between the parents – and this is precisely how God has designed us to be!

However, in describing all the awe and amazement of these events, I deliberately prefixed my description with the words "in one sense", because there is another sense of the delightful development of a first child – and that is a powerful sense of normality and a surety that destiny is correctly at work. I recognise now that this second conviction is the province of the young. It is my opinion that humanity is ideally intended to produce their children when they are young, or perhaps I should correct the word "young" to read "newly mature". At that "young adult" time of life, the awe and amazement of the repro-duction process tends to be accepted with calmness and equanimity. Older parents are more prone to worry about the risks to themselves and the child. As a grandparent, it is now clear to me that the love I have for my grand-children is very powerful – but really quite differently focussed than the love I had for my own children. Life is always a learning process.

My first son, Paul, was born at Good Hope Hospital, Sutton Coldfield on the 20th of April 1971. I was not present at the birth; in those days, the presence of the father at such an event was rare and certainly not encouraged. Furthermore, since ultra-scan technology did not exist in those days, the sex of the baby was unknown until he or she made their way out into the world. Of course it was a very common thing for fathers and mothers-to-be to insist that they did not mind whether the baby was a boy or a girl – and, to a degree, I am sure this was true. But I suspect that most men want to have a son, especially first time around; I suppose it is something of an ambition to replicate themselves in some way. I know that I thought it absolutely wonderful that my first child was a boy. Furthermore, he was so absolutely beautiful, perfect in every way and with wonderful fine blonde curly hair to match my own! Maureen and I were totally enchanted with this wonderful addition to our family – even when he awoke us in the middle of the night – a not infrequent occurrence!

However, there was only one worrying event. After the birth, Maureen found that she had lost hearing in her left ear. We were greatly concerned about this and sought medical attention immediately. A full range of medical examinations confirmed the loss of hearing but no explanation could be offered. It seems that whole or partial deafness is sometimes reported after a time of birth but no treatment or correction could be suggested at that time. Nowadays, an internet search reveals that the word *otosclerosis* is suggested as a possible reason for a sudden deafness but even today it seems that little is known about this condition, which, it is suggested, may be caused by some changes in the fine bone structure in the sensitive parts of the inner ear.

I remember being very strongly possessive towards my beautiful son – I think overly so. In our society, new babies are often paraded proudly and people are encouraged to hold the child to admire him or her more closely. As a very possessive father, it disturbed me profoundly to see my lovely son being held in other people's arms. I wanted to be the one holding him all the time! Looking back on this and remembering my very strong feelings, I feel a certain disappointment in myself; after all, my son was coming to no harm and giving gratifying pleasure to a range of people, some of whom may never have had the joy of holding their own children. Maybe age does bring some degree of wisdom!

Before Paul was born, Maureen gave up her job at Colliers (from where the elderly Ford Prefect had been purchased for £10 years before) and prepared to became a full-time mum. This was the norm in those days, more especially if your husband was frequently absent from home. This was certainly the case in our family. I was very highly committed to my work and to the concept of climbing the accountancy ladder (plus the associated affluence ladder, of course). My working days were very long and there were many occasions when I had to be absent overnight from the Birmingham area, sometimes for more than one night. Maureen's mother, Iris, was a wonderful help to us during the time that Paul was a baby and a toddler; for her, of course, it was a "labour of love" to be concerned with her first grandchild and Maureen was always delighted to have her help and support.

There was, in fact, a time when Hilton's wanted to move the firm's accountancy department to London, which had become the largest and busiest office. I was not in favour of this because it would have meant a family move to London for us. I remember returning home to discuss this proposal with Maureen. She agreed that she had no wish to leave Birmingham. So I declined the proposal to move to London; however, I did have to travel there quite frequently after that.

I think that my great dedication to work and career was typical of the professional generation of those times. While I am sure it has remained so down the following decades, I feel that the situation today is rather worse. Nowadays, it seems that employees are pressured to work long hours whether they wish to do so or not. Although I did not realise it at the time, I was so busy thrusting "upwards and onwards" that it did not occur to me that the frequent lack of my presence in normal home life and activities was detrimental to Maureen and the family. I should have realised this, because my children sometimes asked: "Who is this stranger?" when I appeared in the house. Words spoken in jest but with serious intent, masking a sense of sadness and hurt.

So in retrospect, I now admit that my working life had detrimental elements for me as well as my family. As parents we teach and nurture our children in a whole range of ways. Of course we will not be able to carry out

A Small Piece of Pure Gold

these responsibilities effectively if we are largely absent. In other words, I should have had much more to do with my children and supported my wife better than I did. Money and success are positive factors in one's life but they are not the most important things in the world; I really should have realised that.

Of course Maureen and I were still highly involved with the Church. This was the time that our house fellowship was in full swing and we were regular churchgoers every Sunday. From babyhood, Paul was introduced to the church at Witton and was baptised in 1972 when he was around one year old. I remember it as a lovely service of baptism and, yes, Paul was well-behaved as all members of the Nodding family always are!

Time continued to flash by. I was always busy at work and Maureen was kept fully occupied by a growing and very lively Paul. In mid-1974, we were both delighted when we found that we were to have another child in the following February and we agreed immediately that the time had come to move to a larger house to accommodate the growing Nodding clan. After much searching, we chose a larger detached house in nearby Sutton Coldfield. Moving house is always a time of great turmoil but, eventually, we succeeded in transferring ourselves and our possessions to the new house, which was to be our home for the next 12 years.

Our second son Mark was born on the 15th of February, 1975. The 15th of February was a very special date – it was Maureen's birthday! This was a time of great joy and we were both enchanted by our new son. To mark (!) the occasion of Maureen and Mark coming home, I had purchased a long ornamental wooden trough for the garden and filled it with flowers. This was set up across the front of the house and presented a beautiful and colourful display over the seasons. Maureen was delighted with this beautiful tribute and the trough and its flowers became linked with the arrival of Mark into our family.

Our third child, a girl, was born on the 5th of October 1978. Maureen and I were so pleased to have a girl in the family. She was so beautiful and we all loved her very much. Even Paul (7½) and Mark (3½) loved their little sister – most of the time! However, I regret to say that my mother did not approve of the names we had decided upon for our new daughter, Helen Jane. She advised us forcibly and bluntly that she greatly disliked the name Helen. We should call her "Rosemary", she insisted. The reason for this choice of name was highly improbable.

My mother was a lifelong admirer of Lord Barnard, an important landowner who lived in County Durham, the area where my mother had been born and brought up. In fact my mother's children had already acquired names from Lord Barnard! Lord Barnard's Christian name was "John" and this was the reason that I was christened John. Likewise, my twin brother was christened "Gerald" – the name of Lord Barnard's brother. And, guess what? They had a sister called "Rosemary"; my mother evidently thought this was an excellent and superior name and wished to foist it upon our little daughter. We politely declined her "suggestion"!

Thereafter, my mother steadfastly refused to call our daughter "Helen" and insisted on referring to her as "Rosemary"! I could only regard such an action as dispiriting and I remember that it filled me with sadness that my mother should act in such a way towards her own granddaughter. In the earlier parts of my life story, I have described my mother as a contradiction in many respects; I suppose this is merely another example of the peculiar obduracy that seemed to pervade her whole life.

Notwithstanding my all-too-frequent absences from my family, there were weekend and Public Holiday breaks when we were all together. Of course there was also the joy and excitement of Christmas and Easter, too. At these times, there were parties to attend and relatives to visit, sports and games to play along with food and drink aplenty. Then there were the summer holidays when, each year, my family went for a two week holiday in southwest England. At those times, the car was loaded up to the "gunwales". You may imagine that there was a huge amount to transport! Of course, the youngest child always needed a pram or pushchair and this had to be carried strapped precariously to a roof-rack – no doubt destroying even further the doubtful aerodynamics of the cars of that time. I can remember perilously negotiating the steep and narrow roads of southwest England with a seriously overloaded car!

On holiday, there were sand castles to be built and beach games to be played as well as venturing (timidly) into the ice-cold waters of the sea. At that time, I stood out as an oddity on the beach because I declined to wear casual clothing. I insisted that I was comfortable in my formal shirt and tie. It was something that the family teased me about and was the subject of amused stares from many other beach users. I did not care! Why would I want to be like these sloppily-dressed, half-naked people?

However, I do remember vividly one occasion when my dignity was seriously punctured. Formally dressed as usual, I had decided to walk along a narrow concrete wall structure that led into the sea (presumably for some sort of wave control). As I continued my calm and dignified progress, a larger wave appeared suddenly and broke violently over the wall precisely where I was walking. I was completely and utterly soaked from head to foot! As I turned around, I could see that everyone on the beach was laughing heartily at my plight. I could also see that my own family were rolling about in paroxysms of mirth!

I don't think that even that experience changed my view about how I should be dressed – not at that time, anyway. But all may be pleased to hear that I have now learned how to dress in casual clothes!

8

The Next Decade

My mother died suddenly on the 23rd June 1979 when our daughter Helen was just eight months old. The diagnosis was a deep vein thrombosis in the leg that resulted in a blood clot being carried to her heart and lungs, causing instant death. She had been suffering pain in her leg for a while and had eventually consulted her doctor. He suspected the existence of a thrombosis and said he would refer her to a consultant. My mother did not waste any time – she may well have been convinced of the seriousness of her condition – and arranged for a private visit to the consultant right away.

My sister-in-law Anne (the wife of my brother Gerald) who worked with my mother in the family business, took her to the consultant appointment. After examining her, he said she needed immediate hospitalisation and urgent treatment for deep vein thrombosis. He arranged for her admission to the large City Hospital in Birmingham. Anne took her to the hospital where she was admitted as an in-patient. Clearly, her condition was deteriorating and she was in severe pain.

Anne returned to the family business in George Road and informed my father that his wife was now seriously ill in the City Hospital. It seems that he was unperturbed by this. He replied that he was leaving for London the next day; it was the Methodist Church Conference and he would be absent for a number of days. The Methodist Conference is a yearly event when many hundreds of Methodist Church people from all over the UK meet with their leaders to make decisions that affect the year ahead. Anne repeated to him how ill his wife was and advised him strongly that he should cancel his trip to London. She stressed the severity of his wife's condition, emphasising that it was genuinely life-threatening. He merely shook his head and reiterated that he was leaving for London in the morning.

At the hospital, my mother's condition was thought to have stabilised during the day of her admission but she died suddenly and unexpectedly early the next day. She was just 65. Her husband Bernard, who had left for London that morning, was contacted. Of course, this was not easily achieved, since there were no mobile telephones in 1979. Contact was established laboriously through the minister of the Stockland Green Church, who fortunately had acquired details of the Conference venue in London. With some difficulty, he managed to establish contact by telephone and passed on the sad news. A search for my father was instituted at the Conference and eventually located him. He returned to Birmingham later that day.

My mother's funeral took place on the following Friday. All the family were there, including my sister Angela who had returned from New Zealand, where she now lived. The funeral took place at the Church and the committal service was at the Witton Cemetery nearby.

Losing a mother is a deep and emotional bereavement. Your mother, however many criticisms you may have had of her over the years, is the woman who brought you into this world and so must always be a very special and unique person to you. I was very sad and upset that she had died so suddenly and at such a young age. I had always regarded her as a strong and robust person who would live to a ripe old age, strident, uncompromising and continuing to create waves all around her!

At the same time, I was angry with my father. If you love someone, you do not abandon them when they are seriously ill in hospital. I cannot now remember any specific conversation I had with him around this time but I am sure that whatever words I spoke would leave him in no doubt about my opinion of what he did. Of course, decades have now passed and it is true that time usually has the effect of soothing anger; this has been true for me. More importantly, I have always been constantly aware of the effect of Jesus Christ in my life. This directs me to forgive – and I have done so, long ago. I have forgiven – but not, of course, forgotten.

In the decade before my mother's death, my sister Angela had returned to England several times and pleaded with my mother to visit her in New Zealand. For some reason (I never knew what it was), my mother steadfastly refused and I recall that this upset Angela very much. However, after my mother's death, my father visited Angela in New Zealand several times and the visits appeared to be welcomed.

My father remarried two years later in 1981. His new wife was a widowed lady who was the sister of a good friend's wife. The friend had recommended this course of action to my father; no doubt he perceived two lonely people and thought that they would be good for each other. At first, when they were courting, all was well. After marriage, however, my father returned to all his personal activities (Church meetings, prison visiting, visits to alcoholic families, Masonic activities, etc.) and his wife was often left lonely and neglected. Also, he had promised his wife that they would sell their current houses and buy a new one near her grown-up son but this promise was never kept. Subsequently, when my father implacably refused to change his ways, they divorced.

True to character, I continued my "workaholic" life at Hilton Advertising, travelling frequently around England to their other offices. This meant many days of early starts and very late returns, frequently punctuated by overnight absences. I think that Maureen was rather sad about my all-too-frequent absences from home but she understood that was the nature of my job and always supported me fully. Thinking back, I am so grateful to her for that support and I wonder whether she felt as well supported by me. I really hope that she did. Even with the help of her mother, looking after the ever-changing needs of three growing children cannot have been easy.

In the last chapter, I mentioned that I was focussed upon improving the efficiency at Hilton's in terms of their administrative processes and data handling systems. Traditionally, commercial companies serving customers have simple filing systems which allocate data about each individual customer to single storage points. This is adequate as long as the transactions are simple. However, when there are multiple customers with a range of separate functions in each, simple systems are inefficient at best and likely to become unworkable as the range of functions and the data proliferates. There have been many systems invented to deal with this problem. Probably the best known is the Kardex system, which consists of many shallow trays containing cards, all housed in sliding drawer cabinets. Relevant data is hand-written on to the cards by a range of people.

When I arrived at Hilton's, a Kardex system was in use. An advertising agency is employed to produce marketing material for a customer's product or services and then arrange for it to be seen by the public; this may be as hard copy material in newspapers, magazines, etc., film commercials on television, or voice adverts on sound broadcast media.

At Hilton's, all the financial and other data linked to these functions appeared on the Kardex system which allowed the data to be accessed by staff with relative ease. However, there were problems. Only one person at a time could access, use or update a particular card. Legibility of handwriting could be a problem; there were other dangers too, like entry mistakes and misfiling. In addition, separate ledger systems were needed to coordinate the data and other arrangements were required for special items, such as artwork originals and associated information.

In those days, there were very few computerised systems in advertising agencies and it was my task to investigate how such a system could be installed at Hilton's. I have mentioned earlier my visit to Saatchi and Saatchi in Gloucester when I gleaned a good deal of information by examining their system closely. After much thought, I decided that the only way forward was to acquire some contract programmers and build a system from scratch. A programming company was chosen and Hilton's purchased a state-of-the-art NCR computer which, in those days, was the size of a large filing cabinet. The data storage part of the system consisted of two drawers containing early examples of computer hard disc systems. Each drawer contained two "massive" five megabyte disc systems (a tiny fraction of the data storage capacity available today inside mobile phones!). Also, a copy of NCR's own accounting software was purchased to run on the machine.

Surprisingly, it seems that the programming company did not have a compatible computer in their own offices, so their programmers had to do their development work at our premises. The programmes were written in the COBOL computer language, taking several months to complete. I played a major role in specifying exactly how the programs should perform. After some time, I became so fascinated by the process that I taught myself how to write COBOL programs. This knowledge proved to be very useful later and made our operations at Hilton's much more efficient.

A Small Piece of Pure Gold

As always with computer programming, there were many hours of testing the programs to perfect them. Finally, they worked satisfactorily! However, nothing stands still and there followed years of development and amendment as the computer system extended. In due course, it could even drive a series of linked workstations around the Birmingham office. In addition, the important London branch office was eventually integrated into the system with its own workstation, connected to Birmingham by a very expensive telephone data line which I recall cost around £2,000 per year.

It was during these years that my earlier efforts to learn the COBOL programming language paid off handsomely. As anyone connected with computer programming knows, there is a constant need to correct, update and extend programming. At Hilton's, we found that the contract programmers needed to visit us frequently to amend their computer programmes which were now running all our operations; this proved to be very expensive, since contract workers are never cheap!

With my knowledge of COBOL, I had noted many occasions when the programme amendments were quick and simple, so, instead of calling out a programmer at considerable expense, I decided to carry out some programme alterations myself. I found that my expertise was easily equal to the task; the results were achieved more quickly, easily and cheaply – and my programming expertise was expanded considerably. This was a "win-win" situation for me and the agency; however, I imagine the contract programmers were rather less than pleased!

Meanwhile, my family were growing up fast! My elder son Paul had developed into an enthusiastic and personable boy who was very interested in all things concerned with computers, with which he was capable of doing quite complex and sophisticated things. He was doing well at his junior school and subsequently passed his "Eleven Plus" examinations, so gaining a place at a prestigious boy's grammar school in Sutton Coldfield. Although he seemed to fit in well in his new school environment at first, the reports on his school work began to deteriorate after a time. I can remember attending school Parent's Evenings and being taken aback by the consistently negative comments I was hearing from the teachers; I thought some comments were actually quite insulting.

I came to the conclusion that the teaching methods at the grammar school were not successful for Paul and we decided that he should switch to a nearby college. Here, I recall a period when he was clever enough to be able to achieve good college reports by involving his computer skills to complete home projects, etc. However, as soon as these computer activities came to light at the college, I understand he was told roundly that he should not use his computer. In consequence, his college results rapidly deteriorated. After a year, we decided that he should leave the college and seek work that would develop him appropriately. This proved to be a good decision.

His abilities, personality and capacity for hard work made it easy for him to become employed in a number of jobs where he was able to gain experience of workplaces while pursuing his own computing and other interests. During this period, he continued a strong association with the Church and I was delighted when, around the age of sixteen, he gave his life to Christ. This was a moment of great joy for the whole family.

All these experiences plus his own innate abilities eventually led him to a position with a leading provider of technical infrastructure services for business. Here, Paul was required to complete a range of Microsoft Training and Development packages and he passed all these with ease. Today, he is a highly successful computer consultant, as well as the father of my two incredibly lovely grandchildren, Olivia and Zachary.

I have always been proud of Paul and have recognised his intelligence and ability. I think that his story (like my own) reflects that formal, traditional education methods do not suit everyone; in fact, I suspect they do not suit a significant number of young people, since many very successful men and women recount difficulties and failures at school, especially if these are run on traditional educational lines. In most circumstances, one size does not appear to fit all.

My younger son Mark, 4 years younger than Paul, was always a delightful character. As he developed towards his teenage years, his personality continued to be enchanting. Invariably kind and generous in everything he did, he was very popular with all who knew him. In fact, everybody loved him! Mark never had an academic bent; unlike his brother Paul, he did not attend a grammar school, although he sailed through junior and into secondary education with implacably good humour, achieving satisfactory results. Notably however, Mark had a very unusual gift; he had the gift of compassion, a wonderful gift from God. A few accounts of his actions will demonstrate this clearly.

He was probably around eleven years old when the formed the "Sutton Starvers". He had taken over an old garden shed located at the bottom of our garden. He called this shed his Headquarters. This is where the Sutton Starvers, a small group of his friends, met. These boys would agree to starve themselves for at least a day, in sympathy with the starving of the world. They would then collect money by calling around the houses of the area and donate all the money they collected to good causes. They did not do this just once, or occasionally; this was a frequent and consistent action that demonstrated solidarity with the starving of the world. Mark and his friends acted directly to assuage their suffering. I think this was an absolutely remarkable thing for these young boys to do.

In addition, even when the Sutton Starvers were not active, Mark would still be working on various schemes to collect money for good causes. I remember one occasion when he bought large sack of "Party Poppers" (these small explosive streamers that are set off at parties). He then sold them individually at his school and donated the profit he made to charity. This was merely one example of the many direct acts of his compassion and solidarity with the needy.

Of course Mark, along with everyone else in the family, had a strong association with the Church. In addition, there were Christian holiday activities available at a number of centres across the country and these were very popular with young people. One of these was Capernwray in the county of Lancashire, which had children's holiday courses for 10-14 year-olds. When Mark was in that age range, he went to Capernwray on several successive years and thoroughly enjoyed it. (The Capernwray Centre and Bible School still functions today.)

On one occasion when Mark was there, it seems that a girl in his group had lost her bible and was, of course, very upset. Mark immediately organised a collection of money around his group of friends, purchased a new bible from the bookshop, had all his friends sign it and presented it to the girl. This is yet another example of Mark's remarkable generosity and compassion. Many years later we had occasion to meet the girl who had received the bible. By this time she was training to be a doctor! She told us that she remembered the event vividly and had been greatly moved by Mark and his group's generosity. She still had the bible, she said, and it was one of her most treasured possessions.

It was at Capernwray that Mark gave his life to Christ. The leaders at the Centre impressed upon him that he must tell his parents as soon as he returned home. Mark found it easy to tell his mother immediately after he returned home; he and his mother had a very special bond – a common birthday – and Mark always felt very close to her. He obviously felt more nervous about telling me but I well remember the occasion when he did – it was several days later. Of course Maureen had already told me about his coming to Christ but we agreed that he had to be allowed to tell me in his own time. I was sitting on the patio in the garden, reading a newspaper, when I became aware of Mark circling around the garden near the boundary fences. After a couple of revolutions he gradually approached me and, rather haltingly, communicated his wonderful news. I told him I was delighted and we shared a joyful hug!

I remember also being highly impressed by Mark's dedication to our Church. He had been a loyal member of a Bible Study group that had met routinely at the Church when, for some reason I cannot now recall, it had ceased to function. Mark immediately acted to set up a new Bible Study group (with some adult help) and it met routinely at our house. He called it the "Golden Oldies Club" and it was loyally attended.

Helen was also a delight to Maureen and me. When she was born, we both thought it was really lovely to have a girl in the family. Right from the start, she was notably bright and eager to learn. She went to an introductory school at first and progressed well, then transferred to a junior school in Sutton Coldfield, where Mark was already a pupil. Even at this very young age, she was notably talented. For instance, she wrote a story which was judged to be of such high quality by the teacher that it was submitted to the Head Teacher as an example of very special merit. All her school work was exemplary and her school reports were an absolute pleasure to read.

At the same time, her artistic talents were obvious. On one occasion approaching Christmas, when she became restless in church, she was given a pad of artwork paper and invited to draw the nativity scene that had been set up in the sanctuary area at the front of the church. Helen worked assiduously on this task and the result was so good that the drawing was displayed as "professional" artwork on the front of the next issue of the Church Magazine. In addition, she was a very well-coordinated and graceful little girl. She thoroughly enjoyed attending ballet lessons and became a graceful dancer. Similarly, her excellent physical coordination made her to be a skilled gymnast and she was an enthusiastic and energetic swimmer too.

When I worked at Hilton's, I remember one occasion when I took Helen there for a visit. She was shown around all the offices and introduced to the staff. Knowing that she was reputed to be good at artwork (no doubt I had been boasting!), one of the secretaries asked her if she could draw a picture of a very popular singer and entertainer at that time. Helen set to work and produced a highly impressive drawing. The secretary was absolutely amazed and delighted with the picture of her favourite singer and the drawing was proudly displayed beside her desk for a long time after that. After the visit, I was highly amused when Helen commented at home that everyone at Hilton Advertising had treated me as a "very important person". She had been very impressed by this!

Helen loved and respected her elder brother Mark and always insisted that he was "her best friend". She was always happy to be in his company and tried to be associated with his various schemes. I recall when he set up a "Doozer Society" (inspired by Children's TV's "Fraggle Rock"), Helen was appointed as the Secretary. In addition, she was an enthusiastic member of the "Golden Oldies Club" (Bible Study) which Mark had set up to meet at our house. Finally, when Mark announced that his ambition was to become a superb chef and open a restaurant, Helen announced firmly that her ambition was to be a waitress there!

A Small Piece of Pure Gold

I greatly enjoyed my daughter Helen (and still do!). I think it is natural for fathers to have a close and loving relationship with their daughters. The evidence for this is all around to see. Helen was so clever and talented but this was not the reason that I loved her so much when she was a little girl. I loved her because she was *my* beautiful and wonderful daughter!

In 1987, we moved house again, this time to Four Oaks, on the northern suburbs of Sutton Coldfield. The move was, in fact, only several miles north of our previous location. Our new house was a substantial, spacious, well-designed building sitting squarely in a large plot in Oaklands Road, a quiet cul-de-sac off the main road that connected Sutton Coldfield with the city of Lichfield. It was a very pleasant environment and we settled in there quickly.

This move took us well away from the Methodist churches at Stockland Green and Witton and we decided that the time had come to transfer our memberships to a church that was closer to our home. The Four Oaks Methodist Church, a fine, traditional Victorian building, was within easy walking distance of our new house (less than half a mile) and we decided to transfer to there. Of course, I already knew the minister and many of the members of that church.

I vividly remember arriving at the church for the first time and, before I actually set foot in the building, being asked by the Superintendent of the Children's Department if I would agree to become the Leader of the Junior Department, covering the 8-11 age range. Of course the Superintendent knew that I was highly experienced in this role; I had led the Children's Department at Witton for some time. Even so, I was rather amused to be approached about this before I had even set foot in the church for the first time!

I did agree to become the Leader of the Junior Department at Four Oaks. It proved to be an important post because I soon found that there were many children to look after in the Junior Department, sufficient to require no less than six teachers on duty each Sunday to cover the numbers of 8-11 year-olds who attended. The presence of large numbers of children in any church is, of course, a blessing and a very great joy.

It was also in 1987 that Mr John Hilton (who had taken over from his father as Senior Director of Hilton Advertising) decided to sell the company that had borne their name for so long. Two years earlier, he had set up his own, individual agency and I had been contracted by him to set up the accounting and computer systems he needed. Before selling the Agency, he set about acquiring all the company shares that he did not hold personally. It soon became apparent that he had purchased the shares owned by his father and also the block of shares held by a sister.

This left my own 5% holding outstanding, which I was willing to sell at a fair rate. This proved to be a disappointing disaster. John Hilton employed a top London firm of solicitors who specialised in the negotiation of company sales. They produced a low evaluation of my 5% share of the company, insisting that my shares represented merely a "minority interest". The solicitors who acted for me had little or no experience of such company sales matters and agreed without demur. Having acquired all the company shares, John Hilton then sold the advertising company for a very substantial sum, proving to me that my 5% share had been grossly undervalued. Of course I felt cheated and let down but there was nothing I could do. I resigned from the Agency soon after.

So I was unemployed – but I had already made plans to set up my own company! I now had considerable computer/electronic data processing knowledge to add to my Chartered Accountant qualifications, so I acquired modest offices in Sutton Coldfield. With great efficiency, Maureen joined me to set up the new office, quickly obtaining all necessary furniture and fittings, computers, office machinery, telephones and all necessary consumables. I was then installed as Managing Director and I acquired a Personal Secretary to handle the administration, invoices, etc. Two computer programmers and two sales staff were hired, although, after six months or so, I found that just one computer programmer was necessary. My son Paul also worked in the company for a time.

The first customers of Radclyffe Computer and Management Services were the new owners of Hilton Advertising and a continuing servicing contract with John Hilton's advertising agency. These contracts made total sense, since I had installed and maintained both these systems in the past.

However, the main business of Radclyffe was to sell integrated production and accounting packages to advertising agencies all over the United Kingdom. Our service covered both hardware and software sales and the Company steadily built up contracts in many areas of the Country. A comprehensive brochure advertised all our services and was sent to any advertising agency who wished to develop their services and become more efficient. At this time, I was travelling to locations all over the United Kingdom and, once again, was away from home very often. In due course, our success made it appropriate to move the Company to larger and more modern offices nearby.

Radclyffe had always been a busy and happy place. Our staff total (including me) was only six, so everyone was totally immersed in their own busy activities. The two sales ladies were kept busy on the telephone or preparing brochures or manuals for sending to clients or potential customers. The programmer (as programmers always do) had his head down over his workstation most of the time. Paul, visited him often and they were good friends with a similar interest in all things computing, while my Secretary and I worked together as I led the company forward. Of course we shared coffee and chat quite often and I was always available to sort out any problems.

Meanwhile, although Maureen continued to be the Company Secretary of Radclyffe, she was generally not involved in the day-to-day activities. Instead, she developed her considerable expertise as a florist and specialist flower arranger for a wide range of events (weddings, funerals, parties, etc.). She advertised her services in the local media and responded to any enquiries with an attractive catalogue that included details and illustrations of some of her award-winning flower arrangements. This proved to be a popular and thriving business, run from our home.

There is no doubt that the popularity of her business reflected the very high degree of artistic skill she demonstrated in every single floral display that she created. From time to time, she entered floral competitions and she invariably won high awards. I was always extremely impressed by the efficiency of her business and even more by the beauty and perfection of her work.

A Small Piece of Pure Gold

9

My Son Mark

'**M**ark, we'll need to get you a nice new suit for Grandad's funeral.'

I was not there when Maureen said this to Mark but I imagine that he may have acknowledged her words minimally, perhaps even with a pensive silence. At the tender age of thirteen, this would be his first experience of a death within the family; he had been only four years old when my mother died and so would have no memory of that. Now it was mid-June 1988 and my father had died very suddenly earlier in the month. A totally unexpected death at the age of 79.

He had been at home and, fortunately, my sister Angela was living with him at the time, being on a visit from New Zealand. She later reported that there had been no warning of what was to come. He had left her to visit the bathroom and, a short time after, she had heard the impact of his fall on the floor. When she found him collapsed and unresponsive, she called for an ambulance and then telephoned other members of the family; obviously, she was in a very highly distressed state.

On their arrival, the ambulance staff found that they were unable to revive my father, so they placed him on a stretcher, loaded him into the ambulance and took him to hospital. At the hospital, attempts to revive him also failed and in due course he was pronounced dead. Subsequently, the cause of death was established as a severe heart attack. A sudden death of this type often results in a delay to the funeral, as the law requires some statutory investigations to be carried out. Eventually, the funeral was arranged for June 19th.

Earlier in this book, I have described how my personal relationship with my father was ambivalent at best. Certainly, we never had a close relationship and, through the years, I had found little occasion to love him; I have to say that he did not appear to want love from his own children, only silence and obedience. After I had set up my own household with Maureen, my father and mother visited us from time to time. I recall that Maureen tried her best with both of them (and Maureen was a naturally loving and respectful person) but her success was always limited and the relationship was never easy.

When our children came along – often a tremendous attraction for grandparents – I do not recall that loving bonds were ever formed. Latterly, after my mother's death, my father visited our house alone. However, during every one of these visits, it is my distinct recollection that he never divested himself of his overcoat or even sat down on a chair in our house. Standing in the middle of our lounge, he said what he had come to say and then departed! We thought that his behaviour was very odd and incomprehensible. Furthermore, although the children knew their grandfather and talked to him when he visited, he never appeared to form any meaningful bond with them either.

However, death brings its own thoughts of finality and irrevocable change. It brings thoughts of wasted years and the possibilities of what might have been. This adds to the sadness that is a programmed characteristic of human reactions in such circumstances. We, all my family, sat in the Stockland Green Methodist Church that we knew so well and were disquieted, sad and upset. The church was full; my father had many friends and acquaintances inside and outside the Church. We followed the service faithfully; we sang the hymns, we prayed, we listened to the eulogies. And we thought our thoughts.

Then, after a short drive to the Witton Cemetery, behind the slowly-moving hearse, we stood at the graveside, participating in that awesome and totally alien experience of interment, as my father's body was laid to rest in a burial plot beside my mother. And we, all the family, thought our thoughts.

In the five days that followed, it was inevitable that our minds would flick back to the day of my father's funeral. A funeral is such an hiatus in the normal flow of life. Any time that we paused our introspection and returned to whatever physical reality we were occupying in that moment, we could see that normality was still present; the normality of work, of home, of school or play. In that arena, we could interact normally with those around us. But inevitably, our minds would return us to recollections of the funeral; thoughts of a life on Earth ended and the strange trappings and procedures that inevitably followed. These memories were a part of our lives during these five short days. In due course, we knew that we would change, readjust, return again to "normal" – and that is what would have happened to our funeral memories had they not been totally obliterated by a catastrophe.

I was at work in my office in Sutton Coldfield. I thank God that I was there and not absent in some remote UK location, showcasing the Radclyffe services to prospective customers. The day had been pleasant enough and it was approaching six o'clock when my telephone rang. It was my elder son Paul.

'Dad? Mark has had an accident. He was knocked off his bicycle by a car at the top of our road. He's been taken to hospital. Mum had gone with him. She told me to phone you.'

I froze, my brain racing uncontrollably, trying to understand, to make sense of what Paul was saying. Finally, after an interminable microsecond, I asked a plethora of questions. Paul did his best to answer but his information was sketchy and incomplete. In the end, I gleaned a sequence of events as he understood them to be.

Paul had been playing with his little sister Helen in the back garden of our house. It was 5.15 p.m. on a fine sunny day. They had erected a tent and it seemed that the garden hose had been deployed to spray water on the tent – ostensibly to test its degree of waterproofness. No doubt some of the water was sprayed (by accident, of course) on the two of them as well! Suddenly, they heard a very loud noise, almost like an explosion, coming from the busy major road that runs north from the town of Sutton Coldfield to the cathedral city of Lichfield. This road is only fifty metres or so from the garden. They paused, registered it and then gave it no more thought.

Meanwhile, inside the house, Maureen was working in the kitchen and she heard it too. Later, she told me that she knew *immediately* that it was an accident involving Mark. Without pause, she rushed out of the house and ran up the hill to the major road, where it was already obvious that a road accident had occurred; all traffic had come to a stop and a small crowd had gathered. The residents of the nearest houses were appearing with first aid kits and blankets, etc. A car was stationary in the middle of the road, driverless. In front of it, lay a twisted and broken bicycle, which Maureen recognised immediately.

By the roadside, a small knot of people knelt around Mark, trying to help him. He lay by the side of the road on his back, with his head resting on the raised kerbstone of the pavement. He was unconscious. It seems that the car had struck the front wheel of the bicycle and Mark had been thrown from the machine before the car ran over it.

He had landed heavily where he now lay, striking the base of his skull against the sharp edge of the kerbstone.

Being Friday, this was the day that Mark did his "paper round", when he delivered a local weekly newspaper to the houses of the surrounding area. He had been earning a little extra pocket money in this way for some time. Because many of the houses in this area were quite widely spaced, he had always used his bicycle as transport. On this particular day, I knew that Mark had been excited, eagerly anticipating a favourite event – a weekend at scout camp. He had been due to leave for the camp that very evening.

Clearly, Mark had completed his task and was on the way home; indeed he was only fifty metres away from it. He was emerging from a minor road and had to cross both carriageways of the major road to enter Oaklands Road directly opposite, the location of his home. This was a manoeuvre he had carried out many times and we had always known Mark to be a careful and sensible cyclist, well versed in the rules and dangers of the busy main roads.

The sound of an emergency siren heralded the approach of the ambulance. Soon, the ambulance men were on the scene and were assessing Mark's condition. They told Maureen that he had to be taken to hospital immediately. While they were moving Mark carefully on to a stretcher and into the ambulance, Maureen dashed back home to tell Paul and Helen. She would go with Mark in the ambulance, she told them. Paul was to phone me right away and everyone was to come to the hospital as soon as possible.

Of course I told Paul that I would come home immediately. I then told my staff about the accident and left in a daze of unreality. As I drove along in the busy stream of traffic towards my home, I prayed to God that Mark would recover. Then, another thought occurred: 'Maybe he isn't badly injured, maybe it's just a few bumps and bruises, a bit of concussion.' *Maybe.* I tried to reassure myself, to convince myself of this. I applied all the logic I could muster – to no avail. Then I prayed to God that his injuries would not be serious – but, as I prayed, I realised that this had already been decided by the events at the place of the accident. So I prayed that, whatever Marks' injuries were, he would recover fully and quickly from the effects. 'Maybe it really is nothing serious,' I repeated, hopefully. Desperately.

At home, I was met by Paul and Helen, white with shock and tearstained. I embraced them both; we were all trembling. 'Any news?' I asked Paul.

'Mum phoned to say that he's been taken away for treatment. She's been told to wait. They'll let her know immediately there's any news. She says: "Get Dad to bring you and Helen to the hospital as soon as you can. I'll be waiting for you".'

'Let's all get ready to go,' I said and sent them off for outdoor clothes. 'Maybe he'll be fine,' I kept saying. They said nothing, merely looking at me with large, frightened eyes. Eventually we were ready and I drove the car towards the hospital in Sutton Coldfield. I recall that we were all silent until Paul spoke in a quiet and introspective voice, asking a rhetorical question:

'How can anyone without a faith live through this experience?'

I have never forgotten these words; they were words of absolute truth and words of comfort, too. I felt a great sense of wonder and gratefulness that Paul (and Mark) had been able to give their lives to Christ and so gain the strength that accompanies that miracle of faith.

We were soon at the hospital and found Maureen waiting for us outside the Main Entrance.

'Any news,' I whispered as we embraced tightly.

'Not yet,' she replied softly. 'Graham Benke is here and has been talking to me. He says Mark is in the best possible hands. We just have to wait.' Graham Benke was a friend and former neighbour who was a consultant at the hospital.

'What have they said about his injuries?' I asked.

'The ambulance men didn't think he has broken bones,' she said, 'the car didn't hit him directly. It hit the bicycle and he was thrown off. He was knocked unconscious when he landed. They said he needed a full examination at the hospital and they wanted to get him there as quickly as possible.'

We entered the hospital and reported our presence. It seemed there was no news as yet but we were conducted to a small waiting room where we were alone. After a short time, our friend Graham came to tell us that Mark was going to be put on a life support system. They were arranging for that at the moment, he said, and, as soon as they were satisfied he was stable, we would be able to see him.

So we waited. I led a prayer for Mark, praying to God that he would help Mark to recover from whatever injuries he had received; praying that he would make a good and complete recovery. When I finished my prayer, we all sat in silence, praying, hoping, weeping for Mark and, of course, for ourselves. We were all numb, totally taken over by this terrible catastrophe, unable to think coherently. We just prayed and hoped and remembered. We just waited.

'You can come and see him now.' Graham had reappeared and we followed him silently along corridors and up staircases until we arrived at the Intensive Care Ward, a truly alien place of bright lights, purposeful stillness and humming, bleeping machinery. And there was Mark, lying on a narrow bed, covered by dazzling white covers, motionless apart from the gentle rise and fall of his chest. He was asleep, deeply asleep, his face in gentle repose. He looked so normal, just like I had seen him so many times. Just as I had seen him that morning at breakfast time, eons of time ago. He looked so beautiful. We all thought so.

'Can we touch him,' we whispered. Such places demand whispering.

Graham answered in a quiet voice (not whispering) 'Yes, of course. The machine is maintaining his breathing for him at the moment and making sure he is stable. This gives him the best chance of recovery.'

Very gingerly at first, we touched his hand, soft, warm, normal. Then, increasingly emboldened, we kissed him and hugged him, a sleeping boy who would normally have awakened at our touch. But this time, he did not awake; he did not stir. It was at this point I looked into his eyes, just visible through a tiny parting of his eyelids – and the eyes I saw were dead eyes. A chill passed through me. At that moment, I "knew" that my beloved son Mark was no longer alive.

The news had spread and various people came to be with us, family, friends and neighbours. After three hours or so, the Intensive Care staff told us to go home. 'There's nothing you can do here. Go home and get some rest then come back tomorrow morning. We'll be monitoring him carefully all night.' However, our minister declared that he would remain in the hospital and pray all night for Mark's recovery. We were all so grateful to him. What an incredible thing to do!

We said our "good nights" to Mark and stumbled out of the hospital and into the car. Not long after, we arrived home. Maureen and the children prayed that Mark would regain consciousness during the night. Of course I participated, because God always hears your prayers. However, I felt convinced that we had already lost Mark.

The night was largely sleepless. Maureen wept all night, inconsolable. I tossed and turned, occasionally dozing and then coming to full consciousness again and again as the reality of our situation scythed through my slumber. Eventually, in despair, I rose from the bed, dressed and left the house at 6 a.m. I needed to walk.

In the cool, stillness of a June morning, I crossed the deserted main road where I paused to look intently at the spot where Mark had lain only half a day before. Now there

A Small Piece of Pure Gold

was nothing to see. Just the normality of the unmarked asphalt road surface where his body had been stretched out; just the pitiless, unyielding edge of the kerbstone that had struck him on the base of his skull. Nothing to see but, in my mind, I could see it all, indelibly imprinted.

Then I walked on, not knowing where or how far I was going, my movements automatic, my mind in a confusing unfocussed turmoil. Suddenly, without warning, I felt it. My heart was seized by a mighty hand and held tightly. Physical reality disappeared, obliterated. Time arrested. And God spoke, not in words, not with light or sounds or anything that can be described.

Suddenly, the pressure was released. I had no idea how long God had held me. Perhaps thirty seconds, I thought? But immediately I sensed and understood the clear message he had given me:

'Mark is at peace. He is safe with me.'

In that moment, I was released. Not from the agony of the loss, of course; not from the desolation of the bereavement, or from the sorrow of Mark's absence from this life – for these things cannot be altered or forgotten. I was released from negative catalepsy. I gained power, strength and control which, from that moment on, enabled me to interact freely with people; to talk to them, to give them help and succour. While never forgetting our family's personal loss, it allowed me to speak freely about Mark with pride, admiration and joy. People were amazed – and said so – but I knew this was God's will for me. I knew that this is what he wanted me to do, to sustain Mark's wonderful commitment to this world.

I went home and we made ready to return to the hospital. Before we were allowed to see Mark, the doctors were waiting to speak to us. We sat and listened with sinking hearts. There had been no change in Mark's condition overnight. They thought that there was no brainwave activity. At nine o'clock, they would carry out a special test on Mark which was to detect whether life was present. If there was any activity, this would mean that Mark was alive and had a chance of recovery. If there was no activity, he would remain on life support for the rest of the day and the test would be repeated at five o'clock. If the second test was negative, they would have to conclude that he was dead. They were very sorry but it was absolutely necessary to have this conversation ... Did we have any questions?

Now they had to raise another matter with us. They had noted that Mark was carrying an organ donor card when he was brought to hospital. In the sad event of his death, would we agree to organs being taken?

This was, of course, a deeply shocking question. Yet we were in absolutely no doubt what Mark's wishes would be. He would answer with a resounding "yes"! We discussed the matter and gave our consent. The doctors told us that they would wish to go ahead with that procedure shortly after death was established; therefore, they said, anyone who wished to visit Mark must do so before five o'clock. This news affected Maureen's mother Iris, who was on holiday in Scotland. She was contacted and, by leaving immediately, was able to travel from Scotland and arrive in time to visit Mark in the afternoon.

Of course we spent the whole day with Mark. We touched him, we kissed him, we held him, we talked to him ... and he slept serenely, warm, soft and breathing steadily. The Mark we all knew so well. A great many people came; the ministers of our churches, family members, friends from neighbourhood and church, business colleagues. Also, the driver of the car, a young lady in her early twenties, came with her father. She was extremely distressed and I did my best to comfort her.

All too soon, five o'clock approached. We were asked to leave while they carried out the tests on Mark. They came to communicate the result – I could read it from their faces. They had carried out the test meticulously and they had to inform us that Mark was undoubtedly dead. There was now no possibility of recovery. After a long

A Small Piece of Pure Gold

pause, they reminded us that they would be taking organs in accordance with our earlier agreement. Meanwhile, he was still attached to the life support system as before. Would we like to visit him now?

Of course we did. It was an unbearable time. We each said goodbye to Mark in our own way. For myself, I knew that Mark – the spirit of Mark that gave him life – was no longer there in that body; furthermore that "he" had not been there all the time I had seen him lying in hospital. The Mark I knew and loved was with God in Heaven. I knew that then, in that moment of farewell, just as I know it today. I remember Paul's comment as we were leaving. He looked at Mark and said: 'He's just so … perfect.' I knew what he meant. The accident had hardly touched his physical body; it just extinguished his life.

Of course, the story does go on. Because, even in death, Mark gave life. That is so characteristic of him. His kidneys, his liver and the valves of his heart gave new life and hope to a number of people whose bodies were failing them. How wonderful! We are so very proud of him.

The four days between Mark's death and his funeral were extremely busy ones. Many people came to help and comfort us and we were very grateful for their support. However, having met the driver of the car and her father at the hospital when they came to visit Mark, we contacted them and invited them to visit us. We knew that the young lady was very deeply upset. When they came, Maureen and I had a long chat and comforted them as best as we could, knowing that this is what God (and Mark) would want us to do. Also, we were able to pray together (her father was a Preacher in the Christian Elim Church). I do hope we were able to offer some lasting comfort to them both.

Mark's funeral was at the Sutton Coldfield Crematorium at midday on Thursday 30th June 1988. The service was led by Rev. Laurie Churms, Minister of Four Oaks Methodist

Church and Rev. John Pernu, a close friend of Mark and the Minister of Stockland Green and Witton Methodist Churches. Many people came to mourn and support us, filling the chapel to its capacity.

This was followed at 2.45 p.m. by a Service of Thanksgiving at the Four Oaks Methodist Church. Rev. Peter Nodding (my younger brother) participated in the service. The church was filled to overflowing; it was "standing room only". The huge congregation included Mark's family from far and wide, his many friends from the Scouts, school and other organisations, friends from many Methodist churches in the Birmingham area, neighbours and business colleagues of the family – and seventeen ministers of the Church were present.

In a special tribute to Marks' life and witness, Rev. John Pernu spoke these words:

Mark Nodding was a witness to life at its fullest.
He was a proclamation of joy.
He was enthusiastic, exuberant.
He was life.

Mark was a magnet, a warm human magnet, attracting people,
all sorts of people – young people, old people, any people.
He drew them to himself by first reaching out to t/hem,
disarming them with genuine love.

Mark Nodding was an expression of love, God's love;
love which goes out;
love which is sensitive to other's need;
love which embraces and builds up;
love which invites you to want more.

Just thirteen years, but so rich.
In just thirteen years, what a witness to what we can become.
Just thirteen years – Oh, that we would let
young Mark Nodding be our teacher in life.

He finished his tribute with these words:

The candle we have lit gives of itself as it burns.
It gives light and warmth. It is a symbol of Mark,
and Mark had the knowledge of how to be replenished.

Mark Nodding was a beautiful pebble dropped by God
into the waters of life, our life.
Through Mark, God has sent ripples across these waters,
circles of love which even now are embracing us.

In the family, Mark lives on in our memories. We remember
him vividly. We always will.

10
Miracles

Over the years, I have observed that most people tend to have three categories of activity in their life; these can be categorised broadly as: (1) Family, (2) Work (3) "Other activities". The first is fundamental. We are pre-programmed to live in a family and this is, of course, how human life maintains and renews itself. The second is our means of sustaining our family within the society that surrounds us. The third is wide-ranging and covers everything that an individual does outside the first two categories. In many people, but not all, this could be described as "recreational" activities; however, some people choose to fill this category with outreach work, where they concentrate upon serving others in some way. Of course my analysis is a simplification but there is an important realisation that flows from it. A major change in any of the categories will almost certainly impose significant changes on the other two.

As the Managing Director of my own small company, now approaching my mid-forties, I could analyse my own three categories of activity like this: Family, Work and Church. There is no doubt that these three activities kept me fully occupied. Firstly, a growing family like mine was entitled to much attention and support. Secondly, my commercial business kept me very busy for the largest part of most days. Earlier in this book, I identified myself as a workaholic; even when I was employed by others, my working world was one of very long days and exceedingly late returns to my home. This is why I have already admitted that my frequent absences from family life was the cause of some degree of deprivation for them, although I was genuinely unaware of this at the time. Thirdly, the Church has always been a constant and important influence in my life and I was always fully engaged; there are many ways to be involved in church work and my whole family and I always participated fully. In fact I was a Church Steward of Four Oaks Methodist Church at this time, and so was responsible to the Minister and the congregation for a wide range of aspects associated with the organisation and functioning of that church.

Mark's death fundamentally changed everything for each member of my family. Of course it changed me radically and so impacted on all my personal categories of activity as defined above. The death of a child in the family is an especially agonising bereavement, as it not only removes the person that you love so much but it wipes out all the potential that you have seen developing in that person since their birth. In Mark's case, there had been thirteen wonderful years to observe the development of this potential and this had been a truly awesome experience. Within the family, there is no doubt that Mark's powerful love had "rubbed off" on us and, as a result, we now became more loving and caring towards one another. This also applied to all our other activities and contacts, especially in the Church, because we remembered constantly what a wonderful Christian Mark had been. There is no doubt that his influence in the Church had been considerable; everybody in the congregation of the Four Oaks Methodist Church knew Mark as an amazing, totally loving person.

Anyone who has been a staunch and long-time member of a church will know that there is always a potential for an undercurrent of tension in church matters. This tension can be related to absolutely any aspect of the church; it can appear within any internal or external function or action. It can certainly be generated by discussions surrounding any question of change, be it physical, spiritual or anything in between. Here, the adversaries may well be the "traditionalists" and the "modernists" and it is easy to imagine what their stances will be. Inevitably, polarisation will occur and "camps" will be formed. Furthermore, the complexity of human thought processes may generate many more than just two "camps" about a particular viewpoint. Finally, it is likely also that such disagreements will become suffused with robust passion. This is because each individual church will inevitably play a very important role in the lives of those who are affiliated to it. Thus, views and opinions on church matters are often held extremely strongly – explosively, even!

Nevertheless, it is right that we should be realistic. People (even followers of Jesus!) will never be perfect. We make mistakes. We make bad judgements and the result may be that a tension escalates to become a serious conflict.

Throughout the first half of 1988, before Mark's death, I had seen a steady deterioration in the relationships between a number of "powerful people" in the Four Oaks Church. Invariably, such people have a significant influence on church life. I was not the only one, our whole team of Church Stewards had noted that "camps" and "cliques" had formed and that relationships were being soured by unwise comment and action.

Very regrettably, the reason was related to our Minister's leadership of the Church. While our minister was a very kindly, human and dedicated Christian (remember, he prayed all night for Mark at the hospital, an action of incredible love), it has to be said that his management and

A Small Piece of Pure Gold

organisation skills were wanting. Of course, the leadership of a church is bound up with management and administration; every church needs to be led wisely and well, with all decisions supported by a satisfactory level of efficiency.

In our Church at Four Oaks, this did not happen. The Minister did not appear to recognise (or could not recognise) the importance of his leadership role and so gave it little attention. For instance, he would arrive late for important church meetings where he was the Chairman – or, sometimes, he would not arrive at all! Essential church organisation and administration activities were largely being ignored over an extended period. Furthermore, these problems were insoluble, because church leadership cannot be removed from the minister and given to someone else; the minister is given that responsibility by the Methodist Church Conference, the executive body which guides and oversees Methodist churches everywhere, and this responsibility cannot be transferred. So the Senior Church Steward and his team of Church Stewards, plus all the other elected and appointed Officers of the Church, struggled to keep things operating, against a background of deteriorating morale and disagreement.

Our church congregation was split into two basic "camps" (although there were "sub-camps" within them). The first was populated by those who could forgive the Minister his shortcomings, basically because he was such a lovely, warm-hearted man. That was my own position, although I wished many times that he would become effective in essential leadership matters! The second grouping were those who did not forgive the Minister his shortcomings. It is likely that they would have been affected personally by some aspect of his lack of leadership or efficiency in administration. Then, when time passed and the situation did not improve, more and more dissatisfaction and offence would be generated. This gave additional reasons for members of the congregation to turn against the Minister and, crucially, become even more alienated from the alternative groups who supported him.

I remember that those of us who had some sort of management responsibility in the Church felt a growing sense of despondency. None of us had the power to solve the ever-growing problem and so we observed with despair that the situation in the Church was continuing to deteriorate. Months passed and mid-summer arrived. We perceived that passions were becoming ever more inflamed and that the poison of evil was spreading. Given the elements of the situation, we could not conceive of a solution.

Then my younger son died and God laid Mark's spirit upon the Four Oaks Methodist Church. And everything changed. Instantly.

As I have already said, everyone in the Church knew Mark. Many had seen him growing up, observing and participating in his life of kindness, gentleness and pure love. Now, Mark's spirit changed the ambiance within the Church at a stroke. Miraculously, it released the network of tensions that had festooned the church like a dense tangle of taut spider's webs. Conflict disappeared instantly. Adversaries became friends and the Church proceeded forward in loving concert, just as Jesus Christ would have wanted it to do. A miracle of God's healing delivered through the spirit of my truly wonderful son.

Furthermore, the effect was not short-lived. Such was the power of God in my son Mark that the balm of his love and joy made conflict and tension impossible within any matter or aspect of the Church for the rest of 1988 and beyond. I believe that his spirit was active in the Church throughout that time, such was the wonderful ambiance that prevailed. Then, regrettably, "normality" began to return; new situations to disagree with, new tensions, new adversaries, some who may not have known Mark. I regretted that change but, nevertheless, I was (and am)

A Small Piece of Pure Gold

filled with awe and gratefulness that God used my amazing son for his purposes of love and healing.

Throughout the years, people have asked me what I imagined Mark would have become had he lived to adulthood. I have little doubt that he would have dedicated himself to the caring professions – he had already been a carer for many years. I think that he may well have chosen to be a minister in the Christian religion, where, I am convinced, he would have been wonderfully gifted.

For me, the downside of the transformation in my life that Mark's death brought was that my personal focus transferred from my business to my family and the Church. Whereas before, I had dedicated a large part of my energies to Radclyffe Computer and Management Services, my own beloved company, I now became distracted and disinterested in its operation. My actions within the company lost concentration and, with only five other staff members, there was no manager or supervisor to direct and maintain the focus that is necessary for the continuing success of a small business. Inevitably, business activity started to decline, revenue decreased and overhead costs did not. An inevitable consequence was the development of a growing overdraft in my bank account to meet the costs of my now unprofitable operations.

Given a level playing field, I believe that my business may have survived and recovered sufficiently as my focus returned. Unfortunately, it was around this time that the United Kingdom suffered a short recession (1989-90) and it is a matter of history that many small businesses failed because of this. As the months passed, Radclyffe Computer and Management Services was sinking further into debt because its customer base was shrinking and, in the recession climate, new contracts were proving to be impossible to acquire; I could see that many advertising agencies (my potential customers) were going bankrupt. Because I recoiled from making my loyal staff redundant, salary costs remained high and therefore routine and progressive losses were inevitable in the Company. I suppose it was inevitable that I would receive a letter from my Bank Manager. With a distinctly curt tone, this invited me to a meeting with him to discuss my growing overdraft.

I had always banked with the Midland Bank. This had been the premier bank of the Midlands of England since its inception in the early 1930s (However, I wasn't a customer then!). In the last decade of the 20th Century, 15 years or so after the events I am chronicling here, the Midland Bank was taken over by the banking giant HSBC and the Midland brand disappeared from the streets. Although my business was registered as a Limited Company, I did not differentiate its finances from my own personal resources; this was a matter of convenience when I was setting it up and I had never changed this arrangement. Consequently, my personal bank account was now in overdraft mode to the tune of several thousand pounds – and this negative balance was on the increase.

The branch of Midland Bank where my account was held was within a hundred metres or so from my company offices in Trinity Place, Sutton Coldfield. So, at the appointed time, I gathered the appropriate business and financial records and strolled along to the Bank. There, I was received by a clerk and directed to wait. A finger was pointed towards a line of chairs against one wall. The Manager would see me when he was free, I was told.

I looked around. Everything about this bank was very traditional (by which I mean old-fashioned!). The building was located on a prominent corner of High Street, Sutton Coldfield. It was an elderly purpose-built bank building very much in the traditional style, with an exterior of carved and ornamented stone. It also featured a large and ornate clock, which informed passers-by of the time. The intention of the building's appearance was to announce that here was a solid financial business – completely and utterly dependable, plus trustworthy in every way. The interior had some elements of a sepulchre, dark wood, muted paintwork, frosted glass and whispered conversation. An awesome place, steeped in tradition, respect and money!

Eventually the Manager was free and I was conducted by an acolyte into the presence of the "Great Man". Now, I cannot remember his name. He was unsmiling and very formally dressed as he acknowledged me coldly from behind an imposing, highly-polished desk. With little preamble he invited me to outline the events that were causing my business to require such large elements of borrowing from the Bank.

I marshalled my forces and explained the situation fully, telling him honestly about the effect that Mark's death had had on me and the business. This, I told him, augmented by the recession that had now hit the country, had unexpectedly destroyed the profitability of the business. Before this, I was sure he was aware that it had always been profitable; this evidence was available in the bank records that he held. The need to borrow from the Bank had been forced upon me because, despite the falling revenue, I would not be unfaithful to my loyal members of staff. I pointed out that none of the Directors of the Company were taking a salary from the business at the moment; only the employed staff were being paid. I emphasised that the Company was still very much in operation; it still had a number of active, ongoing contracts and that these would continue to bring in revenue. Furthermore, there was always the prospect that our customer base would increase.

I agreed that the current situation in the Company was not good at present but, in view of the fact that we had previously been a wholly successful venture, I thought it reasonable to forecast a return to profitability in due course. I also mentioned that I had been a customer of the Midland Bank for many years, during which time my accounts had invariably been in credit. Therefore, I concluded, in consideration of all the circumstances, I hoped that the Bank would continue to support me through this time of difficulty.

I sat back in my chair, content that I had explained my position clearly and succinctly. I expected him to agree, probably after a little lecture. In life, it is necessary to put up with such things!

There was silence for some moments. Then he picked up a large, expensive fountain pen and wrote a few lines on a slip of paper, before sitting back in his large padded chair.

'Right, Mr. Nodding. I have listened to you carefully and have studied the documents you have presented. I have also studied your account records. I have to say right away that I do not think your Company has any viable future. So it is my decision that the Bank will not support you any more and there is no question of increasing your overdraft facility beyond its current level.'

He paused briefly and then continued. 'If I were you, I would call in a firm of liquidators and start the process of winding up your Company as soon as possible. To assist you, I have written down the names and contact numbers of two excellent liquidation firms, who I am sure would be able to close down your business with despatch. Furthermore, you should put your house on the market right away and sell it as soon as possible, so that you can zero your outstanding mortgage.'

Now he shuffled all the papers and folders together, sliding my documentation across the desk towards me. 'As soon as you complete these actions, you should pay down your overdraft with this Bank and clear the whole amount. I will be monitoring progress and hope we may complete this business without further personal contact.'

Frankly, I cannot remember what happened after that. I know I was completely shocked as I left the Bank and walked back to my office. I arrived there and sat with my head in a complete whirl. Suddenly I became aware of a small slip of paper that was lying on top of the files I had brought back with me. I picked it up and found the names and contact details of the two liquidation firms given to me by my "friend" the Bank Manager. Suddenly, my mind snapped into operation. In a single, swift movement, I screwed the slip of paper into a ball and threw it into the nearest waste basket. 'I won't do it,' I thought, my mind blazing with determination. 'I won't destroy my company.'

I went home and sat down with Maureen to tell her what had happened. At the end of my account, her face was white with shock. 'Close the business down? Sell the house?' she said, faintly.

I nodded to both her questions but spoke immediately. 'I'm not closing the business down. I've decided that. I believe that things have got to improve again.'

We sat silently for a time. Then she spoke in a small voice. 'But how are we going to live in the future?'

At that moment, I had no answer to give.

In the following days, I found my resolution strengthening. I had a deep feeling of resentment towards the Midland Bank and specifically towards the Manager of the branch with which I banked. I reminded myself that I had banked with them for most of my adult life and that my finances, while never spectacular (especially in the earlier years) were never a matter for concern. Now, after being a consistent and loyal customer of the Midland Bank, they (or, in particular, this Branch Manager) were content to treat me harshly by refusing to support me in my hour of need. I felt angry and betrayed.

Nevertheless I had to decide what action to take. When I analysed my situation again it seemed to me that the Bank Manager's recommendations were draconian in the extreme. My business, although now operating at a loss, had been successful and I had proved myself capable of running such an enterprise effectively. I was sure that his suggestion to close down of the business was a selfish and excessively negative overreaction. I was resolute that I would fight to keep it open. However, it seemed that I would need to take some action to acquire more cash in hand so, very reluctantly, I decided that I should act on his suggestion to sell my house. This was, of course, the last thing I wanted to do, because it had serious implications for Maureen and the family. Nevertheless, I could see no other way to proceed at that moment.

With great regret and heartache, I contacted an estate agent and in due course the house was advertised for sale. It is no understatement to say that my family and I looked with horror and great sadness at the "For Sale" board that was planted conspicuously in front of our beautiful and greatly desirable house in Oaklands Road, Sutton Coldfield.

This was a very depressing time for me, because now I faced the very real prospect of failure; all these years that led to the setting up of my own successful business now seemed to be turning to ashes before me. Never before had I faced a future of deprivation, of true failure of everything I had worked for and invested in. Furthermore, I knew that my family had always looked to me to support them and protect them; now it seemed that I would be struggling to do that in the future. Without my own business, I would need to seek a job – any job that would help to pay my bills. Although I was qualified and experienced in both computer and accountancy fields, I knew that my age would count against me and make it more difficult to achieve satisfactory employment. I knew that the whole family were devastated. I felt completely forlorn and abandoned.

But God had not forgotten me; he had not abandoned me for, within a short time, he sent an angel to transform my life – to transform all the lives of the family. It happened like this.

Not many days after the fateful visit to see the Bank Manager, I was sitting disconsolately in my office when I received a phone call.

'May I speak to Mr John Nodding, please?' a voice enquired.

'Yes, John Nodding here,' I replied.

'Hello, Mr Nodding,' the voice continued, 'this is Alan Vicary, husband of Margaret. I understand that Margaret spoke to you recently at church and I hear from her that you're having some business troubles. Could I come and see you? I might be able to help.'

I remembered immediately who Alan Vicary was. His wife attended the Four Oaks Methodist Church. Now I recalled that she had spoken to me on the previous Sunday. She had said: 'Listen John, I would like my husband Alan to come and see you. I'll ask him to phone you.'

I had acknowledged that this was very kind of her but, in my depressed state, I thought that probably nothing more would come of it. I knew that her husband Alan Vicary held a very senior post in computer and data processing – he was the Managing Director of IBM Birmingham, no less! Now, here he was on my phone, asking if he could come and visit me!

'Of course, Alan, I would be delighted to see you,' I responded. We conversed a little more and set a date and time for his visit later that week.

Afterwards, I wondered how Margaret had known about my troubles. It isn't the sort of thing you broadcast widely! Then I realised where the link had been. My son Paul was very friendly with the teenage son of a close friend of Margaret; they both attended the Church. Paul would have told his friend about the disaster in the Nodding family fortunes. The friend would have told his mother and she would have mentioned it to her friend, Margaret Vicary. Then, Margaret would have communicated the news to her husband, Alan. God moves in mysterious but very effective ways!

I have to report that the visit of Alan Vicary to my office was nothing less than cathartic, a totally amazing experience. I showed him around my offices and introduced him to my staff. Then we sat together for a considerable time while I explained and demonstrated all the facets of my business. I produced and displayed all my records and accounts and showed him how everything had begun to decline, firstly because of Mark's death, when I lost interest in the business and then because of the recession in the country which was still in progress.

Alan listened to me carefully and then examined all my records with great care, asking me a whole range of very pertinent and searching questions. Finally, he sat back in his chair and smiled at me.

'John,' he said, 'you have the core of a very good business here.' These words were music to my ears – and, when I say music, I mean music made by choirs of angels! He went on to say that there was absolutely nothing wrong with the basis or operation of what we were doing. Clearly, it had suffered because of my understandable inattention after Mark's death but he recognised that I understood that fully. Now, as everyone knew, there was a recession in the United Kingdom and no-one knew how long it would last. What Radclyffe Computer and Management Services had to do was to continue its operations, economise where possible without damaging the product and work as hard as it could to gain new clients. He was convinced that the company would ultimately be in profit again as soon as the recession began to release its grasp. He stressed that I should not give up since he was sure we would win in the end.

That meeting transformed me from hopeless depression to vigorous and positive resolution. I remember returning home that evening in euphoric mood! 'Alan Vicary says that the business is sound and that we should not think of giving up. He says that we should keep going whatever happens!' I trumpeted to Maureen. Then I went

A Small Piece of Pure Gold

outside and tore down the "For Sale" sign outside my house. 'We're taking this off the market,' I told her, 'I'll inform the estate agents tomorrow.'

So I returned to work with determined and optimistic vigour and we continued to bump along, rather like a rowing boat making its way across a stretch of very shallow water, floating clear of the bottom most of the time but now and then scraping its keel worryingly on shallower parts! However, there began to be signs of improvement at last, as my renewed vigour and enthusiasm managed to acquire a few new clients. Then, about one month after Alan's wonderful visit, he telephoned me again.

'John, would you be able come and visit me in my office? I would like to hear how you're getting on and I have something else I want to discuss with you.' Of course I was intrigued. I agreed and a date and time was set.

It was very interesting to visit Alan in his spacious and smart offices in Birmingham. I was welcomed warmly and invited to brief him about progress. I reported that his visit to me had restored me to my old vigour and, although my Company was still a shadow of its former self, nevertheless there were now sign of progress and I was satisfied that we were beginning to turn the corner.

Alan was very pleased. Now he leaned forward. 'John, I have a proposition for you. IBM is expanding into Australia and I have been involved in the selection of staff to open a new office there. We have recruited a very good man to take charge of the Australian operation but things are not ready for him to go over there to start work. I would like to send him to work for you in the interim, to help you build up your business. This is exactly the sort of experience he needs; it will be valuable training for him and, hopefully, useful to you as well. John, I stress that this will be at absolutely no cost to you. You are doing me and IBM a favour by employing my man in a training role during this period. What do you think?' Of course I was delighted to accept. It would be very interesting to see what an IBM high-flyer could do! Alan gave me all the details about my new, temporary employee and we agreed that he could start at Radclyffe right away.

My new employee arrived in Sutton Coldfield soon after. It was a pleasure to meet him. He was a large, very energetic and enthusiastic man in his mid-thirties. I briefed him on all aspects of my business and he grasped the essentials quickly. His energy and enthusiasm were very infectious and my staff, who had of course been deeply affected by the misfortunes that had been besetting our work, began to cheer up and be motivated by him. This was very heartening to see and I was very pleased with him.

Not long after, we had a positive contact with an advertising agency in Glasgow and a briefing and sales visit was required. My "IBM Man" (I regret that I now cannot recall his name) was delighted with this prospect and suggested that he and I should go to Glasgow to "clinch a deal". He would be delighted to drive us in his car, he said. So we made the journey to Glasgow and met our prospective customer. Their operation was examined and I allowed our sales pitch to be given by our latest employee; this was delivered with great verve and enthusiasm! Although we were expecting a positive response, the client decided to "think about it" and, in the end, decided not to use our services. Our IBM Man was greatly disappointed!

Nevertheless, he was a significant asset to my business while he was with us. Although he did not manage to capture any new business, his effect on the morale at Radclyffe was greatly positive. I am indeed very grateful to my friend Alan Vicary, firstly for "turning me around" when I was at my lowest and then for providing a high-quality employee to work for me at no cost. This employee was personally responsible for lifting the spirits of my staff and I will always be grateful to him.

In my eyes, I have no doubt that both these men performed genuine miracles for me.

11

A Time to Relax?

The last chapter was entitled "Miracles" because I believe that two very serious problems in my life had been solved in precisely that way. By the end of the chapter, these miracles had solved the grave schisms that had beset my Church at Four Oaks (using my son Mark) and provided a blessèd inspiration for my failing business, in the shape of Mr Alan Vicary and his employee. From personal experience, I know that God sometimes works in this way and I thank and praise him once again for his loving beneficence towards me.

Now it was 1990 and I had reached the mature age of forty-five. So much had happened during the previous two years that I suppose I now expected a period of respite, a very welcome time of recuperation and consolidation. Of course the sudden loss of Mark was (and still is) a source of deep sadness for me but I thought that the three analysed components of my life, that is, my lovely family, my computer and management business and the Four Oaks Methodist Church, seemed to be in a "stable" condition. Basically, I suppose I expected the situation in all these three important components of my life to be relatively quiescent, at least in the near future. Unfortunately, this expectation proved to be completely wrong.

Soon after, my wife began to notice a deterioration in her hearing, affecting her right ear, which had provided her only source of hearing for many years. It will be recalled that she had lost all hearing in her left ear at the time Paul was born. In the autumn of 1989, she consulted our doctor and he referred her to a hearing specialist. The specialist examined her thoroughly and could not find any physical disorder. Eventually, he diagnosed that her hearing loss was due to "trauma", brought on by the loss of our son, Mark. Both Maureen and I were rather taken aback by this diagnosis but we could find no reason to disagree. He then referred her to the hospital Hearing Clinic where she was fitted with a hearing aid to provide correction for her partial deafness.

Time passed and Maureen visited the hearing specialist regularly. Each time, she reported that her hearing was continuing to deteriorate. Each time, he examined her, maintained his diagnosis of trauma and referred her to the Hearing Clinic where they tested the levels of her hearing once again and fitted a new and more powerful hearing aid. After this procedure had been repeated a number of times, I suggested to Maureen that we should seek another specialist opinion because I was unhappy with her continuing deterioration. She disagreed. She would not wish to upset our hearing specialist by visiting another expert, she said. That would imply that she did not trust him. This was very characteristic of Maureen; she was always unfailingly kind and loyal in everything she did. However, not long after this discussion, she suddenly suffered a total loss of the hearing. Attempts by the Hearing Clinic to restore some hearing failed, despite trying the most powerful aids. In the end, we had to come to terms with the sad fact that Maureen was totally deaf.

Although a dwindling hearing capacity had been afflicting her for some time, some degree of hearing ability, however small, is completely different from a complete loss, not only for her but for everyone else around her. Now, our only means of speech communication was by lip-reading techniques. Obviously, Maureen herself had been using a degree of lip-reading for years; all people with diminished hearing develop that skill. In fact I would observe that everyone lip-reads to some degree. For instance, understanding precisely what someone is saying to you is much easier when you are face to face with them and can watch their mouth as they speak; just listening to their voice alone (e.g. telephone or loudspeaker) makes understanding significantly more difficult.

With Maureen, I now had to remember to be in her line-of-sight when I spoke and to make sure that I had her attention. I also had to learn to articulate properly. Obviously, I now had to remember that if I called her from another room in the house, there was absolutely no chance of a response! Of course Maureen soon became an excellent lip-reader and could communicate with people normally. In addition, she could "hear" remote conversations which were far beyond the range of normal hearing people. On one occasion, I remember her leaning over to me and indicating a couple who were deep in conversation some twenty feet away: 'You would never believe what that man just said to his wife!' she said quietly.

Even now, Maureen was still reluctant to consult another expert. In my worry and concern, I spoke to my friend Clifford, who was a retired doctor and a longstanding member of our church. When he heard what had happened to Maureen, he strongly advised that we should consult another specialist. The man he recommended was an excellent Hearing Consultant, he said, who had been a pioneer in the development of cochlear implants, a technology that is a very significant boon to the profoundly deaf.

I persuaded Maureen to agree and a visit to the new specialist was arranged as quickly as possible. After examining Maureen very comprehensively, the consultant was grave:

'Mrs Nodding, I can detect no problem inside your ear but, of course, I can only see as far as the outer part of your eardrum. However, I can see you have a swelling on the right side of your face and I am sure that the deafness you are now experiencing is connected with that. I suspect that you may have a tumour in the area of your inner ear which has damaged your hearing nerves. I want you to see a friend of mine, Tony Hockley, who is a neurologist and a brain surgeon. I am sure that he will establish what is happening in the vicinity of your inner ear and suggest what action is appropriate.' Now that I looked carefully at Maureen's face, I could see the swelling which was causing her face to be slightly distorted at that side.

The surgeon was consulted as soon as we could arrange it and Maureen had various comprehensive tests and scans. A tumour was found to be crushing the hearing nerves of her inner ear; it seemed that this growing tumour had been the cause of her steadily deteriorating hearing and was the reason for her subsequent deafness. Furthermore, the tumour was still growing and was now in danger of obstructing a carotid artery, which is the upper part of the body's major aorta system; if the carotid arteries are blocked, death follows inevitably, we were told. Therefore, an operation should be carried out as soon as possible. Once removed, the tumour would then be analysed and he hoped it would be found to be benign. He emphasised that this would be a very complex and lengthy procedure.

The surgery was arranged to take place in the Birmingham Queen Elizabeth Hospital on a Sunday in November 1991. I was told that this was the very first time a surgical operation would be carried out on a Sunday. We were reminded that the operation would be a long procedure, at least three hours. In the event, the surgery lasted eight hours. Afterwards, the surgeon reported that, despite all his efforts, he had been unable to remove the whole tumour. He said he had been operating in the brainstem area and had to be extremely careful. Mercifully, the excised tumour was found to be benign and so would not spawn secondary tumours in other parts of the body. This was a great relief.

However we were advised that a further operation would be required after Maureen had recovered from the surgery she had just undergone. At that second operation, he hoped to be able to remove the remainder of the tumour. This would be give her the best chance of a good outcome; however, he did not think she would regain her hearing because of the damage inflicted upon her aural nervous system. Obviously, Maureen was unwell immediately after the operation, since surgical activity in the vicinity of the brain is bound to have a profound effect. In addition, because the inner ear was involved, her balance was greatly affected. Nevertheless, she improved slowly and was able to return home for Christmas.

At the beginning of 1992, we saw the surgeon Tony Hockley once more. He was anxious to complete the total excision of the tumour and the second operation was set for late in January. This time, the operation lasted an interminable twelve hours! Finally, the surgeon appeared, looking completely exhausted. He sat down with me and told me that, despite multiple efforts, he had been unable to remove all of the tumour once again. To do so would have been too dangerous for Maureen and he decided that it would be unwise to proceed. This time, unsurprisingly, Maureen took longer to recover from this second operation. She found that her balance had been greatly affected and needed to be confined to a wheelchair for two or three months afterwards. Nevertheless, after that very slow recovery period, her balance improved and she was then able to resume walking and return to a semblance of normal activity.

Obviously, this was a time of great worry and upset for my children and me. When she was admitted to hospital for the first operation, it was clear that Maureen was in a very serious condition and there was a very real possibility that she might not survive. Certainly, she would not have survived if the tumour in her brain had continued to grow; that had been made very clear to me.

I was so grateful to Tony Hockley for his immediate diagnosis of her problem, followed by his herculean efforts to cure her and restore her to good health. Brain surgery is indeed an extremely delicate process and I was only too well aware that the surgery itself can cause irreparable (and fatal) damage. The surgeon reported to me that he had successfully achieved the excision of most of the tumour; to do more was likely to cause a negative outcome, he said. Because of that state of affairs, we understood that the tumour was likely to regrow in due course. It seemed that a forecast of "due course" was not possible. Of course the family and I could rejoice that Maureen was very much "with us" again.

At this time (Spring, 1992), the recession that had caused so many small business to fail was now over but the recovery from such events is characteristically slow. Nevertheless Radclyffe Computer and Management Services had weathered the storm (with the divine intervention described in the last chapter) and, although progress was slow, I was able to keep the business solvent. My son Paul had joined the firm in 1991, and, with his interest and experience in all things computing, added to his very pleasant and outgoing manner, he was proving to be an asset. Although the recent past had been very difficult for me – Maureen's hearing problems and subsequent surgery had of course been a constant worry, I had been able to retain sufficient focus to maintain my business and take advantage of the improving economic situation in the Country. So, thankfully, there were no problems in that important area of my life.

Unfortunately, the same could not be said of the Church during the time of Maureen's illness. The time had come for a new minister to take over the Four Oaks Church. The new minister was a truly delightful man who was very effective in all aspects of his function at the Church. I was a Church Steward at the time of his arrival and I recognised that he would be an excellent leader for us all. I remember that his very first sermon in the church was on the subject of "conciliation". This was an appropriate and very powerful call to the congregation and it did impinge positively on the situation. Importantly, I noted that everybody appeared to like and respect our new pastor and I am sure he would have had a very good and lasting effect on the Church had he been able to serve his expected five-year term. Regrettably, this was not to be because, within months of his arrival at the Church, he became seriously ill with a very aggressive form of cancer and, after an illness of only several months, died in the Spring of 1990.

Unsurprisingly, the Church was now without a designated minister for five months or so, although we were grateful that a retired minister supported us during this period. However, everyone looked forward eagerly to the arrival of the new minister in September 1990. At this time, I was still a Church Steward and so had responsibilities for the organisation and functioning of the Church, including participating in the welcoming arrangements for the new minister.

At the appointed time, the new minister arrived with his family and moved into the Church manse. I think it fair to say that I have never met a Methodist minister quite like him. We all know that human beings come in an almost infinite range of varieties and they then impose their principal characteristics upon the actions of their daily lives. However, society also plays a role in human behaviour. Obviously, Methodist ministers are selected and trained to follow the particular paths of Methodist ministry and worship, so that an essential conformity is overlaid on whatever personal characteristics and convictions they may have. Thus, while there are always variations in individual ministerial techniques, these are expected to fall within the general rules of the Methodist Church, which are set out in various Church publications in the form of mandatory Standing Orders.

Our new minister was a tall and notably flamboyant character, in demeanour very forceful and rather impetuous. These characteristics are quite unusual in a person whose mission is to serve God and the Church. At the same time, I recognised that he was a very intelligent and energetic man whose Christian and biblical knowledge was very comprehensive. During the first six months or so that he was at Four Oaks, his services in the church were generally appreciated, although it is certain that some of the more traditionally-minded members found him a little too extravagant for their taste!

However, I am of the opinion that he put some very effective ideas into practice. For instance, rather than arranging for the usual "agape meal" in the Church, (this is a reflective and intimate coming together of the congregation, usually held during Easter week), he proposed that separate, smaller agape meals should be held in the houses of Church members, with attendances of around ten people at each. This would be much more intimate and meaningful, he claimed, and more akin to the original actions described in the Bible. With great vigour, he was able to arrange that 220 church attendees would attend one of twenty-two separate agape meals held at the homes of individual members. My own house was one of these and every person who attended this agape meal confirmed that the intimacy of the smaller group made the experience much more effective and spiritual.

It was not long after this that I became the Senior Church Steward and so acquired many additional responsibilities for the functioning and organisation of the

Church. In general terms, everything seemed to be going fine but little did I know what church problems would soon appear!

The time of Pentecost is the time when Christians celebrate God's Holy Spirit being poured out on his people (the dramatic biblical account is in the Acts, Chapter 2). At the services around Pentecost, the minister set about imposing a very "charismatic" character upon all the church services he led and soon it became clear that he intended to continue in this overtly charismatic vein.

While the makeup of Methodist Church services is quite varied, they are generally not based on charismatic principles but rather on the comprehensible, solid and rather informal practices set out by its founder, John Wesley in the 18th Century. Nevertheless, it is also a fact that Pentecostalism grew out of the Holiness Movement that was in turn inspired by John Wesley's *A Plain Account of Christian Perfection*. While it is true that Methodist ministers and preachers will introduce some "spiritual" elements into their services, the more extreme facets of charismatic churches (e.g. being "slain by the spirit" and rendered semi-conscious) are not practised. However, our minister now made every service at Four Oaks overtly charismatic, to the delight of some and the absolute horror of the rest!

Unlike most Christian churches, where the minister of a church leads virtually every service, the Methodist Church has always had a tradition of rotation. So although ministers are attached to a specific church and concentrate most of their activities there, they will only conduct a proportion of services at that location; at other times, they will preach at other local Methodist churches in the area while another Minister or Preacher colleague comes to preach at their church. A published rota allocates the services accordingly. Thus, our minister's charismatic services were imposed not only upon Four Oaks but on other local Methodist churches too, generating the same mixed opinions within their congregations.

Inevitably, the charismatic services caused a deep divide in the congregation at the Four Oaks Church. Those who reacted positively to the new charismatic services revelled in their extremely emotional nature; this group was highly supportive of the Minister and insisted that the Church was very greatly improved. Those who reacted negatively (the majority, including all the Church traditionalists) were appalled by the "antics" that were now routine in their Church and were determined to return it to their sense of normality.

While it seemed that our minister was more than happy to bathe in the adulation of his followers, he peremptorily dismissed the objections of those who were opposed. Of course, many of the objectors were very long-standing members of the Church who were not going to be cowed by the minister! Worryingly, the Church Steward team was also split in their opinion; of the six Church Stewards, three were greatly in favour of the minister's approach and three were against. This was very unfortunate, because the Church Steward team needs to be completely united as they serve the church and the congregation. This fundamental difference of opinion made my leadership and coordination roles very difficult. My own views about the minister were ambivalent; I liked him and respected his knowledge and dedication but I did think that the constant imposition of his charismatic ideas was too extreme.

As the Senior Church Steward, many angry and bitter complaints came to me, either directly or through my Church Steward colleagues. Because their church always means a great deal to those who attend (especially if they have been doing so for half a century or more!), passions were often highly inflamed and there were occasions when very aggressive and hurtful words were directed personally at me. As a Senior Church Steward, you need to be robust (by which I mean tough!) and stay calm in the face of upset and high emotion; you need to realise and accept the depth of frustration that people feel about their beloved church and try to react serenely, while concealing your hurt. Of course, there was little that I could do. As Senior Church Steward, I was the representative of the congregation to the Minister. It was also my duty to support the Minister in his work. When I spoke to him and raised the question of the congregation's distress and opposition to his very charismatic approach, he just brushed me aside casually.

I also became aware that complaints had been raised about our Minister's visits to other local churches. Members of their congregations had complained to their own ministers about the charismatic and extreme nature of his services. Of course, there were also those in these churches who approved greatly of these services, so the other ministers were likely to be confused about what action to take and probably decided to "monitor the situation" – which is an acronym for doing nothing!

Like most mainstream Christian churches, the Methodist Church has a hierarchical structure. Individual churches are grouped into a "Circuit", led by a Superintendent Minister. The Circuits are then grouped into a "District", led by a District Chair and the individual Districts are linked to the "Methodist Conference", the central office of Methodism in the United Kingdom where the President and the Methodist Council are located. The complete Methodist organisation structure, which is of course much more complex than the brief sketch set out above, is referred to as the "Connexion of Churches".

Therefore, above individual church level, the next person in the chain of command is the Superintendent Minister, who coordinates all the churches, ministers and staff of his or her Circuit. After a while, the Four Oaks Church members who were opposed to their Minister and had had their approaches to him rebuffed began to write formally to the Superintendent Minister.

The Superintendent Minister was a wise and highly experienced man.

At this point, formality and regulations began to enter the frame. Obviously, the Superintendent Minister needed to establish the full facts of this case over an extended period. It will be recalled that the Four Oaks Minister had groups of enthusiastic followers in every church, as well as those who were opposed. After some time, the Superintendent Minister invited me, as Senior Church Steward of Four Oaks, to a meeting with him at his house to discuss the problem.

I wondered who would be attending this important meeting with the Superintendent Minister and was greatly surprised when there were only the two of us. He and I spent a considerable time discussing the problems and he asked me very many searching questions. In conclusion, I gave him my opinion that the situation at Four Oaks was now very bad because a significant number of "powerful people" were now vociferously opposed to what the Minister was doing. The Superintendent Minister was silent for a few moments and then he said: 'John,' he said, 'I think we'll have to go for curtailment.'

I had never before heard of this term and asked him what it meant. He explained. 'Basically, it involves a decision by the Methodist Church to "curtail", cut short, a minister's 5-year term at a particular church, because of unacceptable behaviour of some type. This behaviour can cover many things but it's a way of pulling unacceptable ministers out of a particular appointment at short notice. As you may imagine, it's an extreme measure that is used very rarely. But, in this case, I think it may well be justified. What do you think?'

I must say I was shocked by this extreme development but I recognised that the situation at Four Oaks could not be sustained. Our Minister had served less than one year of his five year term and there was no way that I could envisage his continued presence for another four years.

A Small Piece of Pure Gold

'I agree with you,' I said simply, 'what happens now?'

'I will consult with the District Chairman,' he said. 'I am sure there will need to be some sort of hearing, involving you and many others. I'll let you know as soon as I can. Meanwhile, you might like to look at the regulations on curtailment; it's all set out in CPD.' I knew the publication to which he referred. It is a weighty document concerned the organisation and regulations of the Methodist Church. CPD means "Constitutional Practice and Discipline (of the Methodist Church)". After the meeting with the Superintendent Minister, I did look into the CPD publication at the sections on "Curtailment" and I must say that I was dismayed by the brutality of the regulations I read. It seemed to me that there was no compassion or mercy to be found there; just cold, hard legalism.

In due course, the Four Oaks Minister was called to attend a meeting that would judge whether curtailment should be applied to his tenure. The meeting was led by the senior staff of the Circuit and District. I and a good number of other members of the Four Oaks congregation were invited to attend and some members from other churches in the Circuit were present also.

The proceedings opened with a brief statement about the purpose of the meeting. Then, everyone present was invited to contribute their viewpoints, the majority of which supported curtailment. When it came to my turn, I merely stated that our Minister's overtly charismatic approach had caused considerable discord in the church and there continued to be significant and very worrying strife. Therefore, I could not see how this situation could continue for years to come because it would be extremely detrimental to the Four Oaks Church.

After all the evidence had been given, the senior staff withdrew to consider what action should be taken and the result was a unanimous decision that curtailment should be applied.

In response, the Four Oaks Minister stated that he refused to accept the decision.

I was very shocked by what had happened. While I accepted that the Minister was totally unsuitable for my church at Four Oaks, I questioned whether the procedure to remove him needed to be quite so harsh. However, I suspect that these procedures probably date back into Methodist history. Nevertheless, having listened to all the evidence, both for and against, I did think that the decision to apply curtailment was totally fair.

Characteristically, our Minister returned to Four Oaks and proceeded to ignore the curtailment decision of the authorities, which had been carried out in accordance with the Methodist Church Discipline Statutes. In total defiance, he continued to preach in the Four Oaks Church in his usual charismatic style. Of course it was not long before this flagrant disobedience became known to the authorities. I was not party to what happened then but, no doubt after discussions in "high places", it became known that a second, even more formal process of curtailment would now take place. I understand that a special tribunal sat some months later and the curtailment decision was upheld. Our Minister left Four Oaks shortly after.

Everyone in the Church now hoped that there would now be a period of stability and serenity, since the previous two years had seen the tragic and unexpected death of one minister, followed by the extreme turbulence that was associated with his flamboyant successor. Acknowledging the problems that had beset Four Oaks, I know that the District Chairman searched for a new Minister who would be capable of appeasing the church and healing the schisms it had experienced. I think that his strategy was to choose someone who had totally opposite qualities to those of his immediate predecessor.

This strategy worked to some degree but I now observed that this new Minister's rather controversial

A Small Piece of Pure Gold

interpretations of scripture plus a generally rigid, uncompromising stance did not find favour with many Church Members. Thus, I do not think that total healing was ever achieved during this period. Churches are very sensitive organs and it takes highly gifted leadership to achieve a true Christian balance.

By the end of 1992, with my term of office as Senior Church Steward completed, I felt at long last that I could begin to relax to some degree. When I looked back at the years 1988 to 1992, I could see with absolute clarity that it had been an absolutely horrific time for me. Everything in the three "components of my life" had been beset by catastrophic problems. In my lovely family, I had lost a wonderful and much-loved son to a road accident and my wife had been struck down by a life-threatening illness that had been extremely difficult to treat and imposed deafness and serious mobility problems for her. My computer and management business, the pride of my life and our sole means of financial support, had almost been wiped out and my Church had been through a devastating period of unrest and schism.

Now, mercifully, I felt I was settling back on a more even keel. Maureen was well recovered and in good spirits, my business was improving steadily and I hoped that my Church would return to greater normality. Of course, Mark's absence from our family was, and will always be, a deep sadness for all of us. Nevertheless, in the following years, we were generally happy and fulfilled and I remember with great pleasure my 25th Wedding Anniversary in September 1993, when Maureen and I invited our many friends to large party. It was an occasion of delightful fellowship and happiness.

In my speech to the assembled company (a triumph, meticulously videoed of course!), I was able to review Maureen's and my married life together, emphasising the great joy and happiness that had been a constant feature of our long time together but acknowledging also the sadness that had also come into our lives, too.

So life was stable and serene; but Maureen's illness was not finished with her.

The tumour returned in 1995.

12

The Rolling Stream

Time, like an ever-rolling stream...

(Isaac Watts: Psalm 90)

Apart from the continuation of her total deafness, (which was, of course, a great frustration for a fine musician like her), Maureen had managed to have over three years of remission from her very unpleasant illness. Of course, there had been regular visits to her consultant surgeon. Each time he asked many questions about her health and examined her very carefully, then recommended that we should visit him again in six months or so. He continued to warn us that we should expect the tumour to regrow and that further surgery was inevitable.

Now, in 1995, she began to experience the onset of worrying symptoms again. She was once again experiencing serious giddiness and her lack of balance was making it increasingly difficult for her to walk without support. We immediately visited Tony Hockley, our surgeon. He said that everything pointed to the regrowth of the tumour to a critical size and he arranged for Maureen to visit the hospital for immediate investigations. Various scans were carried out and these confirmed the presence of the tumour once again. After examining the evidence, the surgeon advised that surgery should be carried out as soon as possible; this would be a similar operation to those done by him in the past, he said. We should not delay.

Maureen was admitted to hospital not long after. Within days, in a very long and painstaking procedure, the tumour was excised in the same way it had been before, using a heated probe which enabled small parts of diseased material to be removed piece by piece. In addition, because there was an increasing danger of fluid accumulating in the skull, it was deemed it necessary to install a "shunt" – a tube that would drain any accumulation of fluid from the cranium and channel it to her stomach.

So my family and I experienced once again the long and agonising wait while this complex operation took place – another 12 hour surgery in the operating theatre. Eventually, the surgeon appeared and advised me that he had accomplished as much as he could. Once again, it had been impossible to remove every part of the tumour because of its involvement with the brain stem. He had installed the shunt and was satisfied that this would provide a good measure of safety for Maureen. With such serious and repeated surgery, a build-up of fluid in the brain is very likely and this could be very injurious, he told me.

After the surgery, Maureen was taken to Intensive Care and was looked after there for several days until they were happy that she was stable and beginning to recover. We were able to visit her but she was very drowsy or asleep for most of the time. The children and I were very relieved that the operation was over once again. We knew that her recovery would be slow and that she would be kept in hospital for a number of weeks. As she recovered slowly, I saw that her facial nerves had been affected on the right side and she was now unable to close her right eye completely. It was explained to us that this was not unexpected; she would

A Small Piece of Pure Gold

be helped by the insertion of a small piece of pure gold into the upper eyelid; the weight of this metal would assist the damaged nerves and weakened muscles to close the eye normally. This was done subsequently and proved to be a successful solution.

Eventually, the wonderful day came when Maureen was discharged from hospital. Naturally, she found that she was very weak and her balance had been affected very badly. It was necessary to return to the use of the wheelchair once again and make use of it for an extended period, probably around four months or so. As a naturally energetic person, she did not like to be confined to a wheelchair but had to recognise that it was the only way to be able to move around! Eventually, the body provided its wonderful healing and she found her balance returning once again. Gradually, her ability to stand and walk returned, although she always required a degree of assistance which I and the family were happy to provide.

As she recovered, I realised that this third operation had modified her personality. Where before she had always been a person who lived to serve others with vivacity, enthusiasm and caring determination, she had now changed to become a gentler and more introspective person. In addition, her voice had changed, not only in its tonality but in the way she chose words to express herself. To me, the "new" Maureen was as delightful as the "old" Maureen – but in a fundamentally different way! I know this may sound rather peculiar, but I found myself "falling in love" with my "new" wife all over again!

Although she was now weaker and more unsteady, Maureen could still contribute richly to the lives of all around her and she spent her days doing precisely that. She had her own small car and could visit friends or join in a whole range of daytime church activities. Always a very compassionate and loving person, Maureen would be the first to visit those who had suffered bereavement or had other reason to be afflicted by difficulty or sadness. This was something that she had done throughout her life and her diminished physical condition did not change that. Although she could not continue her commercial business as a professional flower arranger, she still retained her extraordinary skill in this art and was able to contribute enthusiastically to the flower displays in church. During this period, I remember that she organised a stunningly beautiful Flower Festival at our church and this was greatly appreciated and admired by many visitors.

So once again, all the family greatly enjoyed Maureen's return to heath. We all acknowledged that she now required more help than before – for instance, although she still went shopping, we needed to be there to help carry the purchases! We all hoped that her period of remission from the effects of the tumour would be long-lasting.

At this time, Maureen and I felt generally optimistic. We accepted that the tumour would probably regrow and that further surgery would be necessary in due course. For my part, logic suggested that since the three previous operations had been successful, there was a very good chance that this sequence of events could continue. Of course I accepted that the operations affected Maureen quite badly at the time but I knew I would always continue to support her through the difficult times when she felt unwell or had lost her normal mobility. The years that followed were a happy and fulfilled time in our life.

After the recession of the early 1990's had slackened its negative grasp, my computer and management business had been building up well and by 1996 I had forty satisfied clients on my customer list. In recent years, an expanding company called Evans (Lichfield) Ltd had become an important customer of mine. They were a manufacturer of cushions and other similar products such as bean-bags. The company had started from very small beginnings. The owners were a married couple who started designing and making cushions at their home in the city of Lichfield and then selling them from a modest market stall. Their products became very popular and the business had expanded rapidly.

By the time I was contracted to work with them, they had become a medium-sized company, employing over 100 workers in a factory and office complex on an industrial estate in Lichfield. The management and control systems were manual and basic; they had not kept pace with the rapid expansion of the company. For this reason, the Joint Managing Directors had contracted me to develop and install modern computer and data-processing systems which would deal with all aspects of their substantial commercial operation. Over a period of time, my company successfully developed and installed everything that was required.

In 1996, the Directors, Mr and Mrs Evans were so pleased with the work I had done for them that they proposed I should join their company in the position of Financial Director. In fact, this was fortuitous. Coincidentally, in a review of my own business operations, I had concluded that I was approaching a time when fundamental changes to my own operations were required. The Radclyffe systems and products were based on the obsolescent COBOL computer programming language which was being replaced by a range of more modern developments, specifically designed for the considerably faster and more sophisticated hardware of the day. I had recognised for some time that it would be necessary for my company to carry out major, ground-up reprogramming of our systems and products; this would mean investing significant amounts of time and money.

After a thorough review of my personal position, I decided that this was an ideal time to sell my company and accept the Evans offer to become their Financial Director. This would allow me to diversify my work into new and more modern areas of management and data processing without huge personal cost. However, I was determined to look after my loyal staff and I always kept them in the forefront of my mind when I was making the sale arrangements.

In the end, I sold my company's operations and products in 1996. My buyers took over my products, systems and advertising agency clients. I made it a condition of the sale that my long-time programmer Steve transferred to my buyer's company to continue his work. My son Paul had his own list of clients which he had built up during his time with my company. He was able to obtain a good position at a large UK and European provider of technical computer support for business and agreed to transfer his personal contracts to them. My other staff obtained satisfactory jobs elsewhere in the local area. I then sold my office building and, thus, Radclyffe Management and Computer Systems ceased to exist. Of course this was a big change in my life but I looked forward to new challenges in my new position.

In fact I worked with Evans for the next ten years, until I decided to retire. The company continued to develop and I ensured that the systems used were optimally developed to meet all their needs efficiently. In addition to my own development work, I managed the Accounting Department, as well as all the staff who dealt with Stock Control and Production in the factory.

In 1997, it was time to change ministers once again and our new minister was Rev. David Easton, a positive, highly energetic and very compassionate man who was so successful at the Church that he stayed with us for the next ten years. David Easton was (and is) a delightful man who was very effective in the Church and popular with all. It is a measure of his energy and compassion (and that of his wife Joan) that, having brought up their own children, they then proceeded to foster a succession of children. The manse, situated adjacent to the Church, was always a very busy (and noisy) place!

Important events were also happening in my family. My daughter Helen had been attending the Bournville Art College in Birmingham and starting to develop her artistic career. In 1997, she was awarded a place at the prestigious Central St. Martins University of the Arts in Kings Cross, London. This university is a world leading centre for art and design education. I well remember driving Helen to London where we settled her into her student accommodation there. While the university's student accommodation in the Halls of Residence were adequate, I thought they were hardly ideal for her so, the following year, I bought a house in the London Borough of Stratford, so that Helen would have more suitable accommodation to live in. She was able to live there as my tenant, sharing with several other girls from the university.

Three years later, she graduated with an Honours Degree in Fine Arts. She followed this up with a position at the internationally famous Victoria and Albert Museum in Cromwell Road, London, where she gained a great deal of experience working through the many departments of that famous artistic institution.

In that same year in June, my son was married at the Four Oaks Church and the ceremony was conducted by Rev. David Easton. This was an occasion of great family joy. The formal wedding reception was held at Aldridge, the area in Staffordshire where the bride had been brought up. A second more informal reception was held subsequently in a marquee in my back garden in Sutton Coldfield.

As this happy year was proceeding towards wintertime, I noticed that Maureen was becoming increasingly unwell and, in November, she had to return to the wheelchair that she disliked so much. Obviously, we arranged to consult our surgeon Tony Hockley as soon as we could. The familiar routine was followed once again and the return of Maureen's tumour established. By early December, she was in hospital again and the operation was scheduled for the 12th. This time, Maureen was occupying a private room at the hospital and she had the photographs of the children lined up on the window sill where she could see them. It was clear that Maureen's health was deteriorating and I was anxious for the operation to be over and her recovery period to start. I suspected that her recovery would be slow but this did not concern me overmuch as I knew I would deal with whatever problems she had while she proceeded along the road to recovery.

The day of the operation finally arrived and I was informed once again that it would be a very long procedure. In fact, she was in the operating theatre for twelve hours, a similar period to the earlier procedures. When it was all over, the surgeon came to inform me that he had been unable once again to remove the tumour completely; this, he wanted me to understand, would certainly have been too dangerous for Maureen. Although she had been deeply unconscious during the surgery, he said that her body had been reacting physically at times to his probe; when he saw that this was happening, he knew it would be extremely unwise for him to proceed any further. Finally, looking very grave, he went on to tell me that Maureen was now much weaker than before and, inevitably, her recovery from this latest surgery should be expected to be very slow. 'In fact, John, she may not be restored to the level of recovery that we have seen before,' he concluded.

By the next morning, Maureen was conscious but clearly very weak. Furthermore, it was obvious that the operation had caused her further physical damage as she was now paralysed down the whole of her left side. When I asked about her recovery from this paralysis, the surgeon's reply was distinctly equivocal: 'Control may or may not come back, John. I really don't know if the nerves will regenerate. But if movement doesn't return, she will not walk again.'

Of course, in the family, we all hoped and prayed that movement and control would return to her left side. After

A Small Piece of Pure Gold

all, we had seen how she regained movement and balance in the past, hadn't we? The body is capable of wonderful healing, is it not? We recognised that our reassurances to each other were not said with a great deal of conviction, however.

The days passed, on one hand an almost seamless high-speed blur, peopled by the many friends who came to visit us; on the other hand, however, time had become turgid, a painful leaden-footed progression of interminable minutes. Somewhere in this peculiar time continuum (I know not when), Tony Hockley took me aside and told me:

'John, I need you to know this. If Maureen gets a chest infection, we will not resuscitate. Do you understand what I am saying?'

Yes, I understood these words – and yet I did not. They were describing an action of such gigantic finality that my mind was totally unable to conceive of them. So, outwardly, I acknowledged his advice with some sort of "normal" response, while inwardly I felt totally numb – cataleptic, frozen, blank.

Now it was 19th December. When I arrived that morning, the anaesthetist came to see me:

'Mr Nodding, I am afraid that your wife has acquired a chest infection. We are treating it as best as we can but she is not responding particularly well.' I remember being glad that the rest was unsaid. Maureen was fully conscious but weak and we spent the whole day together, with various friends coming to visit. Later that day, I had a long conversation with Tony Hockley. I can only remember one thing about it. As I was about to leave him and return to Maureen, he looked me straight in the eye and said:

'John, you do realise that Maureen has only a few days left, don't you?'

I think he must have recognised the extent of my refusal to contemplate the inevitable – and I have to say that he was right. Somehow, although the upper layers of my thought processes had begun to break down into some form of acceptance, the deeper levels of my consciousness were still frozen in a sort of disoriented and traumatised optimism.

There was no doubt that Maureen's condition was becoming worse. Quite suddenly I became convinced that she would leave us at exactly 5.15 p.m. on 24th, December, because our beloved son Mark had been killed at 5.15 p.m. on the 24th of June, ten years earlier. Maureen and Mark shared the same birthday and I knew how close their relationship in this life had been. 'That's when Mark will come to take her to Heaven,' I thought. I was so convinced that I would be right about this that I shared my conviction with Paul and Helen. I remember that they received this prediction thoughtfully and in silence.

The 24th December arrived. 5.15 p.m. came and went and Maureen did not leave us. When my astonishment had finally left me, I was joyful. Now we could spend Christmas together! Maybe she would get well again! Why not? People have miraculous recoveries sometimes, don't they? I remember vividly that Maureen now wanted to go home for Christmas! She instructed me to gather up all the family photographs that were set up on the window sill, so that they could be taken home and restored to their proper places. Despite my euphoria, I knew that this was out of the question and I persuaded her gently that she had to stay in the hospital, because this was the very best place for her to be.

Christmas Day arrived. The family gathered in that room with Maureen and we had a wonderfully joyous time together, a time filled with love, laughter and tranquillity. I remember vividly that Helen's Christmas present to her mother was a beautiful red chiffon scarf. Maureen was absolutely delighted with the scarf and insisted that it was the best Christmas present she had ever had! She draped it around her head and wore it throughout the day. At the end of that wonderful day, we all felt "the peace of the

Lord." It was a truly wonderful experience and I thank God for these hours of love and happiness. I also have to mention an act of extreme love towards our family. Our Minister David Easton came to visit us on Christmas Eve and Christmas Day, despite the considerable responsibilities of his own wife, children and foster children – and he came again on Boxing Day, too.

Maureen was clearly weaker on Boxing Day. There was no doubt that all the festivities of Christmas had been a strain on her. Paul and Helen came to be with her during the day. I remember that I spent some of the day reading passages from the Bible to her and holding her hand. I insisted that Paul and Helen should leave so that they could attend Christmas/Boxing Day parties that evening. I felt strongly that they were in need of a time of normality. However, as time passed, I felt that Maureen was sinking and I knew I should not leave her. Calling for the nurse, I asked if the hospital could provide a bed for me, so that I would be close to Maureen during the night. Subsequently, I was informed that this had been arranged.

By the evening, Maureen was asleep and I sat there reading the Bible and praying. As the clock approached 10.15 p.m., I became aware of the silence in that room, broken only by Maureen's soft and gentle breathing. There was no other sound; my own breathing seemed to be noiseless. Suddenly, I felt as if this room was the world and that I was held comfortably in it, almost in a form of suspended animation. As I registered that, Maureen's quiet breathing changed. Suddenly, she took four, deep, long breaths and then ceased breathing. Immediately after the fourth breath, I was positively aware that something was leaving her.

I almost saw it. I almost heard it, I almost felt it. In that microsecond, I knew unquestionably that her spirit had just departed from her body. Her soul, her life force, her *ruach (Hebrew)*.

I called for the nurse but I knew without doubt what she would tell me. She came immediately and shone a small torch into each of Maureen's eyes.

'She's gone,' she said quietly. This was just a physical, worldly confirmation. I knew that the beautiful and wonderful person that was Maureen had departed to go to another place, to be with Mark and her father and many, many others. And, looking across at her, I saw that her face, which had been so distorted by the effects of her disease, had regained its beauty.

The nurse had called Tony Hockley, who was still working in the hospital. He came immediately and led me away to his office, explaining that the medical staff now needed to attend to Maureen. He comforted me in my grief, although I cannot recall any words he said or any conversation we had. I know that I felt grateful love for this wonderful man, who had done so much to cure Maureen of her illness. I knew he had been responsible for giving us wonderful years of life together.

The next two weeks were a blur; days that somehow had lost the structure of time within them. Yet, there were so many things to deal with. The funeral to be arranged. People to tell. Many friends to speak to. Huge detail upon which to make decisions. And everything was dealt with, although I do not know how. All my family and friends rallied around to help and comfort me. I was the centre of the maelstrom; the apparently calm middle of the circulation of a torrent.

Maureen's funeral took place on 7th January 1999 at the Sutton Coldfield Crematorium. The service, which was conducted by my friend and Minister, Rev. David Easton. was beautiful. The Crematorium Chapel was filled to overflowing. Everyone knew and loved Maureen. I had invited my surgeon friend Mr. Tony Hockley to attend the funeral and he had said he would come if he could. In the event, he not only attended the funeral at the

A Small Piece of Pure Gold

Crematorium but came also to the Service of Thanksgiving for Maureen's life, which was conducted subsequently on that same day at the Four Oaks Methodist Church.

The Rev. David Easton led the Service of Thanksgiving, which recalled the many great achievements of Maureen's life. He thanked God for her Christian witness, her selfless love and her constant caring compassion towards all people. Several hundred people filled the church to capacity.

Everyone loved Maureen.

13

The Advent of Solitude

So now, for the first time in my adult life, I was alone and bereaved. Mark's death in 1988 had of course been an absolute agony but, although the death of a loved one acts to turn every individual into an almost impregnable island of grief, a surrounding cluster of family members means that the agony may somehow be assuaged to some degree – perhaps implicitly rather than overtly. When Mark died, all the other members of my family were still living at home and the presence of loved ones is always a blessing and a comfort; their normality and familiarity is a balm.

Now it was different, totally different. Maureen, the love of my life, was gone. My eldest son, Paul, was a married man with his own range of family responsibilities; he no longer lived "at home". His new family status had effected an appropriate and proper transformation in our relationship; the close unit of "father and son", while still a physical reality, had nevertheless changed into a different entity. However, Paul still lived in the local area and I was grateful that I saw him quite frequently, along with his new wife. By contrast, my lovely daughter Helen lived and worked in London. She came to visit me when

A Small Piece of Pure Gold

she could but her life was no longer in Sutton Coldfield. Of course, it had not been for several years.

In that time after the bereavement of a dearly-loved one, life is lived within a cocoon of numbed desperation. I suppose this is the mind's attempt to reach back into the happiness that was the glory of yesterday. At first, day-to-day activities are carried out in a strange and confusing facsimile of normality (for life must go on, mustn't it?), accompanied by a vast mental void that somehow cannot be refilled or repaired. Then, as the days, weeks and months pass in a speeding blur of strange, pointless activity, the central core of one's being gradually slows its all-pervading, frenetic activity, and begins to seek some sort of calm; a new and different semblance of stillness.

In these early days, I can remember a few outcroppings of significance.

I was able to acquire the small piece of pure gold that had made it possible for Maureen to close her right eyelid after her third operation in 1995. Subsequently, I made a pilgrimage to Birmingham's famous Jewellery Quarter, where I arranged to have the gold fused into the slim platinum band of Maureen's wedding ring, expanding its circumference so that I could wear it on my little finger. The jeweller carried out my instruction beautifully and it was a great comfort for me to be able to wear Maureen's ring as a constant reminder of our wonderful marriage of thirty years.

Earlier in the book, I recounted how a good friend of mine, Clifford, a retired doctor and fellow Church member, had insisted that Maureen should change her hearing specialist to one that he recommended. This had resulted in the rapid and correct diagnosis of her problem and had led immediately to the series of essential operations that followed. After Maureen died, Clifford contacted me and asked if he could speak privately to Paul and Helen about the death of their mother. Paul and Helen agreed and I recall that he came to my house. The three of them spent some time alone and afterwards, both Paul and Helen told me that their discussion with him had been very comforting, meaningful and helpful.

Some time after, I recall that Clifford was taken seriously ill at a Church Meeting. By the time the ambulance arrived, he was unconscious and seemed to be sinking towards death. The ambulance staff diagnosed that he was suffering a heart attack and immediately applied resuscitation. This was successful and, after a period of hospitalisation, he recovered fully. I was delighted – but Clifford wasn't! In fact he was very displeased. In the most forceful terms, he told me that he had not wanted to be resuscitated and he was very annoyed with the ambulance men for bringing him back to life!

It is said that time is a great healer. I know why that adage is used with respect to bereavement. In a sense it is true but, for me, I would prefer a different saying to describe the healing that one receives in bereavement. I would say that "people are the great healers", because it is through their love, compassion and dedication that some semblance of normality is gradually coaxed to return. In my case, I count many people who helped me to function in my new and solitary state and, gradually, assisted me to diminish and deal with my paralysing grief.

Of course my family rallied around and helped me, not only the Nodding family but Maureen's family as well. My mother-in-law, Iris, had always been a marvellously supportive person in our lives and now she focussed her support for me. I was also very grateful for the support of two of Maureen's uncles who lived some distance away. I enjoyed many pleasant and relaxing visits with them. My many friends from the Four Oaks Church also supported me, especially the members of our house fellowship, which had been functioning continuously throughout Maureen's illness and was still fully active at this time. (Today, the fellowship still meets regularly at my house, although I no longer take a leading role.) Also, I thank my

A Small Piece of Pure Gold

many friends from other churches who have kept in touch with me, as have the many people whom I met through my business activities.

However, I really must single out one very special friend who has always been an exceptional tower of strength and love to both Maureen and myself. Like many men of my generation, I had never needed to "look after" myself throughout the span of my married life. In addition to her constant love and wonderful companionship, Maureen ensured that there was always splendid food for me to eat, clean clothes to wear and a marvellously spick and span house to live in! Now my beloved wife was gone and I was cast adrift on this lonely island called bereavement, quite incapable of looking after myself. Into my gulf of despair stepped my wonderful friend Diane Forsythe.

In this book, I have mentioned Diane just once – near the beginning of Chapter 1. She was a close family friend who, back in 2014, confirmed an allegation of my son Paul that I was changing rather quickly in several physical respects. They both said that I was "slowing down" and that there had been a noticeable change in my voice, which had become weaker and more husky. In fact, Diane had been a wonderful constant throughout a large part of my life. I first met her when she was just a little girl!

In my teenage years, I have already explained how I had become a Christian who was greatly affected by the inspirational Rev. Stanley Johnson, the Minister of Stockland Green and Witton Churches. Stanley motivated his new young Christians to take special responsibilities for the children in his churches and I was one of those who was "sent" to be a Youth Leader at the Witton Church, which, in those days, had many children who attended the young people's activities regularly. So, it was as a teenage Youth Leader that I first became acquainted with Diane, who I recall as an energetic little girl in a pink dress! Of course, Maureen Harris, my future wife, was at that time a young teenage girl in that same church and was already acquainted with Diane as a regular attendee of the children's Sunday School.

Throughout the years, both Maureen and I continued to know Diane as a fellow member of the Witton Church, which we all continued to attend well into adulthood. As reported earlier, Maureen and I were married in that Church in 1968 and, subsequently, Diane was also married there to our friend, Terry Forsythe. As the years passed and children swelled both our families, we became firm family friends and shared many pleasant times together at each other's houses.

In the late 1980s when Maureen became ill, Diane immediately became a very regular visitor to our home and helped us in so many ways. She remains an impressively energetic person who is filled with great love and compassion for all who are in need of practical and psychological assistance; for many years, there has been a wide circle of people who have been wonderfully supported by Diane. She is greatly loved and an inspiration to so many.

When Maureen died in 1998 and my life collapsed around me, Diane immediately started to visit me regularly and supported me in every way, taking over all the things that had to be done in the household. In 2015, when I was diagnosed with MND and began to deteriorate physically quite quickly, Diane instantly became my principal support, helping me in every way and staying constantly in touch. She comes to my house almost every day and telephones me frequently.

I am so grateful for all the things that Diane now does for me. My life would be very greatly diminished without her.

It is very common for people who have been bereaved of a beloved partner to become depressed. However, I would claim that I am not a person who sinks easily into depression. I seem to find support in the spontaneous kindnesses I see so often in people all around me. In

A Small Piece of Pure Gold

modern life, it is often asserted that many people are rushing around so frenetically that they become totally absorbed with their own problems and do not ever focus on others. I think this is a superficial view. If you look around you, at any time and in any place, you will see acts of kindness and compassion taking place. In my opinion, such acts and attitudes are an essential component of what it is to be human – and everyone (yes, I do mean everyone!) participates in such acts at times. God equips everyone in this way.

Of course, the loss of Maureen was a devastating sadness for me but I can remember only one short period of what I will define as "depression" in my life. This happened around six months after Maureen died. I have already described what my life was like earlier in 1999, the routine of daily life swirling around the central confusion and numbness of my being, followed by some gradual healing and acceptance as time flowed on. Now, suddenly, I was beset by a week of depression. I did not want to live any longer without Maureen. I remember lying in bed and praying earnestly to God to "take me". Having done so, I fell silent and waited to see what would happen.

As it turned out, God did not "take me". At the end of that week, I concluded that God must still have a purpose for me in this world. Of course, in Christian obedience, I accepted his judgement and, immediately, my depression vanished. Thinking about it afterwards, I knew that God's answer to my prayer had not been delivered in majestic, echoing words (like a scene in a Hollywood blockbuster movie), or even sent directly to my brain in some subliminal way but it had been communicated to me through the wonderful human beings who surrounded me, unfailingly radiating God's love and nurture through their voices and actions. I have long known that this is how God often chooses to work in this world. Today, this remains my conviction.

When Maureen was alive, we had made provisional plans to visit New Zealand in the millennium year to visit my sister Angela, who had lived there for some time. I now proposed that we now should go together as a family and so, in February of the year 2000, Helen, Paul and his wife joined me in a visit to New Zealand. For a very special reason, we broke our journey at Sydney, Australia for three days. This was to meet up with a very special person who now lived in Australia – the Rev. John Pernu, who was the Minister at the Stockland Green Church when my young son Mark died. Earlier in this book, some of the beautiful and comforting words that he had said at Mark's funeral have been included and I have always been deeply grateful to him for these words.

In fact, John Pernu now lived in Melbourne, which was a nine-hour car drive away from Sydney. On the day we arrived, he left his home about midnight and, after driving 600 miles throughout the night, arrived at our hotel around 9 a.m. After greeting us, he announced his intention to show us around the "sights" of Sydney and its surroundings, brushing aside my recommendation that he should rest first. We had an extremely pleasant day with John and reminisced about our former life when he was in the UK. Of course, I took the opportunity to thank him once again for the wonderful and inspirational words he had spoken at Mark's funeral. He responded that he had only been telling the truth about Mark.

I was very sorry to hear that he had given up his ministerial position in the Church for personal reasons, because I had known him to be a very fine Methodist minister. It was extremely kind of John to make such an arduous journey just to renew his acquaintanceship with us and then, despite the tiredness he must have felt, to serve as our tourist guide throughout the day. John Pernu is a wonderful man who served God with true dedication and compassion. I am sure that he does this still. I will always wish him the very best in his life.

After our pleasant break in Sydney, we were soon on our way to Auckland, New Zealand, located in the north-western part of North Island. My sister Angela met us at the airport. Very conveniently, she had her own minibus to transport us all to her home because she was now a contracted agent for a local taxi organisation who coordinated private hire transportation in this part of New Zealand. After settling in at Angela's spacious house, we had a very happy family time all together, recalling many events of our life in the UK. During the following two weeks, Angela took us to see the many of the "sights" of North Island, where there are many interesting and unusual things to see, like the amazing areas of hot springs that produce bubbling hot (sometimes boiling!) pools of water in a range of very surprising colours.

I recall also that she took us to visit one of Maori settlements. This proved to be a very memorable experience, especially for Paul. The settlement had been set up as a tourist village and the indigenous people were determined that we should experience all aspects of their somewhat unusual culture. I am sure that everyone has seen (on TV, or maybe on the rugby field!) the fierce Maori greeting dances where a line of warriors appear, liberally daubed in white spots or stripes and charge noisily forward waving large spears and making extremely grotesque and terrifying faces. Well, in real life, I can tell you it's even more frightening, especially for the lone person who is chosen to have the honour of greeting the chief of the dancers, who is made up to be the most fierce and terrifying of all the company. And the lone person who was given the "honour" to greet the chief ... was an unsuspecting Paul!

So there we all were, with Paul isolated out front, fully briefed to hold his ground and greet the chief. The dancers appeared and advanced forward threateningly, finally rushing forward terrifyingly and giving every indication that they would kill all of us! Let us say that it was a very memorable experience, especially for poor Paul! And, yes, we had to rub noses, too! It is what you might describe as a unforgettable experience, one that was very nice when it was over!

After two weeks, my family had to return to UK but I stayed on with Angela for another four weeks or so, enjoying her company and soaking up many more interesting sights around Auckland. It was during this period that I decided I should see South Island as well. My absence would give Angela some respite from my constant presence and allow her to return to her normal activities.

New Zealand is a fascinating country with a wide variation of climate from north to south, because the two islands extend over thirteen degrees of latitude (35 to 48 Degrees South). This means that, although the overall climate is largely temperate, the north of North Island (including Auckland) experiences subtropical weather in the summer season, while the southern regions of South Island have cold winters with temperatures often falling well below freezing. South Island is significantly more mountainous than North Island, with many rugged peaks that become deeply snow-covered in winter. Only 25% of New Zealand's total population live in South Island, despite its significantly greater land area as compared to North Island.

Angela told me that there were coach tours that ran from Auckland all the way to Invercargill, the most southerly town of South Island. Such tours would cover all the sights along the way. She directed me to a travel agent whose premises were in the Sky Tower, a dramatic, tall structure over 1000 feet high which offered panoramic views over the Auckland region.

I admit that I approached the prospect of this tour with some trepidation. On past excursions, I had always been accompanied by Maureen and, like all married couples, we were a comfortable "island", nested among many other travelling couples. Now, for the first time,

I faced the prospect of being a solo tourist – the odd one out among a community of many pairs. However, I plucked up my courage, found the travel agent's shop at ground level in the Sky Tower and marched in to make my enquiries. After a review of all the available tours, I judged that there was an eleven-day bus tour which appeared to meet all my needs. It would travel to the southernmost parts of South Island, taking in all the tourist sights and then return us back to Auckland. As a bonus, a visit to Stewart Island was included; this large island around 20 miles off the southern coast of South Island, is a wild and dramatic place populated by fewer than 400 people. Most of its population live in Oban, the main settlement named after the town on the western coast of Scotland – the island and its inhabitants obviously have a strong Scottish connection.

In the event, I had a wonderful time on this eleven-day tour, visiting a whole range of very interesting places throughout the length of New Zealand. Furthermore, there was absolutely no problem with my individual status. Although most of the people on the tour were in pairs (as I expected), I was made most welcome by absolutely everyone. As we all travelled on, I realised something that was very valuable for my future life; it is usual for single people to talk freely to one another while people in pairs tend to be rather more reserved. I think that the reason for this is simple; the pairs have each other to socialise with and so will tend to have less need of others. This was a wonderful and reassuring realisation for me, one which I have proven to be true time and time again. Not only was the trip throughout New Zealand a wonderful experience from a tourist point of view, it actually released me from the nagging, almost subliminal personal worry that I would be forever solitary and ignored. Furthermore, this trip released the "travelling bug" within me!

Finally, I must include an account of my meeting with a Stewart Island sheep farmer when I took the opportunity of visiting that awesome and remote place. This very friendly and pleasant man had been born and brought up on Stewart Island and had lived all his life near the settlement of Oban. He said that his ancestry was Scots. Some time before, he had made an epic tourist journey to the UK and had greatly enjoyed all the tourist sites of London and other parts of England. However, he was of course determined to visit Scotland as well so he made sure that he joined a bus tour that would include the Scottish town of Oban in its schedule. For obvious reasons, he wished to experience and, no doubt, photograph the place that gave its name to his own Stewart Island settlement. I imagine he would be planning to give illustrated lectures when he returned home!

So his Scottish bus tour got underway and followed its specified schedule. The visit to the town of Oban was the very last stop on the tour. In the late afternoon, as the coach was bowling along the Scottish Highland roads, the driver made an announcement over the PA system.

'Ladies and gentlemen, I'm sure you have all noticed that, because of various delays, we are now running significantly late. So I do not think we have sufficient time to visit the town of Oban. I propose that we now return directly to the starting point of our tour. I am sorry for this change of plan and I hope that this will be acceptable to you all.'

The coach was filled with the hum of many voices as people digested this news and discussed it with each other. Listening to the discussions around him, the New Zealand farmer was appalled to hear that most people seemed to be resigned to the loss of their visit to Oban. As far as he could hear, his fellow tourists seemed to be willing accept the driver's proposal. The farmer was deeply shocked. Now he would not see and experience Oban!

'NO!' he roared as loudly as he could. 'No, it is NOT acceptable. I have travelled ten thousand miles, all the way from New Zealand, just to visit Oban! We must go to Oban.' Then he moved to the front of the coach to discuss

A Small Piece of Pure Gold

it further with the driver. As he did so, other travellers on the coach began to support the New Zealand farmer.

The driver's decision was reversed. The coach visited Oban for its scheduled visit and the farmer's cherished ambition was wholly fulfilled! I thought this was a marvellous story. I congratulated the farmer on his steadfastness and told him that I was very glad that his ambition was properly met.

Back in Auckland, I was very grateful for Angela's kindness to me at that vulnerable time in my life and, before I returned to the UK, I was pleased to be able to use my business experience to help her with a particular problem she was having with the purchase of a property in Australia. Angela told me that she intended to retire to a very attractive city in Australia called Gold Coast. This is situated in Queensland, on the Australian eastern coast just south of the major city of Brisbane. It is a hugely popular tourist area which is famed for its extensive sandy beaches. The area is also famous for its system of inland waterways and canals. Angela had visited the region several times on holiday and, on one of her visits, had seen that an excellent beachside property was offered for sale. The owner of the property was an elderly man who lived there alone. After the necessary inspections, etc., Angela decided to buy the property at an agreed price and the contract was drawn up. In Australia, as in many countries (but not England) house buying and selling is an instaneous affair; once the contract is drawn up and signed by buyer and seller, the deal is done.

Angela was delighted that she would now be the owner of this excellent property until the elderly man's son appeared on the scene and announced that the house was not for sale; his father, he said, had changed his mind. Of course, it was immediately pointed out to him that the house was contracted to be sold and the matter was concluded, just awaiting the agreed financial transaction.

The son was implacable in his view and refused to allow his father to complete the contracted sale. Angela took legal advice and was advised to take the matter to court. She was told that the law was clear – there was a valid contract in place and the seller could not change his mind. Knowing how complex these matters can turn out to be, I offered to help Angela with the paperwork. I wrote letters for her and helped her with the other paperwork.

The wheels of the law often grind slowly, especially if one party in a dispute is determined to be as awkward as possible. However, Angela persisted, knowing that she was in the right, and, although it took over three years for the courts to find in her favour, she eventually won the case. A satisfactory by-product of the 3 year delay was that the agreed price for the property was maintained while the market value of Gold Coast properties soared!

As yet, Angela has not retired to her dream home and rents it out at the moment. She was grateful for my support and expertise in this matter and I was delighted to be able to help her achieve a most satisfactory outcome! In a subsequent visit to Angela, during the time of the protracted court case, Angela and I had a holiday in the city of Gold Coast and I was able to view the location of the property that she had agreed to purchase. It was an absolutely beautiful house, ideally located. I could appreciate fully why she wanted to retire to this breath-taking place.

14

Perpetual Motion

After I returned to the UK, I suddenly found that I had developed a very abnormal thirst, that is, I felt a constant physiological need to drink and was drinking vast quantities of water day and night. I admit that I thought this was rather strange but, as I was feeling quite normal in all other respects, I did not pay a great deal of attention to this change in my intake of water. However, my friend Diane soon noticed my great thirst and advised me to go to my doctor, because, as she pointed out, this change in me had been sudden and very marked.

Obedient as always (!), I visited my doctor and various tests were arranged. Subsequently, when I returned to the doctor, he informed me that the tests had shown that I had developed Type 2 Diabetes, a metabolic disorder that is characterized by abnormally high blood sugar levels because of a relative lack of essential insulin being produced in the body. It seems that the sudden onset of a great thirst is a common symptom of this disorder. He told me that I would need to start a medication routine and change my diet to avoid sugar. Once I had established both these routines and my thirst had diminished, he said, I would be checked periodically to ensure that my insulin levels were within normal tolerances. By following the treatment, I was grateful to find that I was soon able to return my body to an acceptable balance and return to my normal life.

Nevertheless this first onset of adult illness was a sobering shock. Like many other people, I had lived the whole of my life with my body coping manfully with whatever stress I placed upon it and succumbing to only minor and temporary ailments like colds. I suppose I thought that my life would stay in that healthy mode for ever – or, at least, until "old age" came upon me. I now had to come to terms with and accept a degree of mortality that was unknown to me before this event.

Shortly after this medical interlude, I recognised that the time had come to sell my large house in Sutton Coldfield and move to a smaller, more suitable property for my single status (small, but not too small!). Before Maureen died, we had discussed moving house and she was keen to move to a bungalow. She had an ambition to move to a particular road in Sutton Coldfield, a very pleasant place where many good-quality bungalows had been built. However, when we surveyed the market, there were no bungalows for sale in that road (inevitably!). Of course the matter was shelved when Maureen became ill again.

After Maureen died in December 1998, a number of good friends advised me strongly to "do nothing" until a whole year had passed. By "do nothing" they meant: "Do not make major changes to your life. You're likely to make mistakes that may be detrimental for you. Instead, see how you're feeling in a year's time." It seems that this is very common advice that is given to a bereaved person in the early weeks and months after a loved one is lost. I can understand why. I have already mentioned the desperation and emptiness that one feels at that time and I am sure it would have been all too easy for me to indulge in radical changes to my life in a spasmodic effort to defeat the sadness and despair that pervaded my existence. It seems that I was surprisingly obedient to this advice – although I don't think I am thought of as a particularly obedient person. However, perhaps I recognised the common sense that my friends were offering to me; perhaps also I sensed the fundamental dangers of what hasty and ill-judged decisions might bring to me.

The specified year had now passed and I fully accepted that a move from my large family home was appropriate. Thinking back to the previous discussions I had with Maureen, I felt that a bungalow-style property in Maureen's chosen road (within easy walking distance of the Four Oaks Methodist Church) would suit me very well. There would be an additional comfort for me if I achieved this, as I would be fulfilling Maureen's stated ambition. Sadly, when I contacted the estate agents, I found that there were still no suitable properties for sale in that road; it has always been popular with house buyers in the area, the estate agents told me. However, I saw in the local newspaper that there was a bungalow for sale in an adjacent road and took the opportunity of viewing it with my very good friend Diane. We both liked the house and agreed that it would be a very suitable property for me. Of course, like most home owners who want to move, I had to sell my own house first and it seems that nothing ever happens quickly when you want it to! For many weeks, the "For Sale" picture of my house was advertised in the local newspaper alongside the picture of the very house I wanted to buy! Very frustrating!

It took four very long months to sell my house. All that time, I hoped that the bungalow I wanted would not be sold. In this respect, I was very much in luck. When I finally found buyers for my house, I immediately acted to purchase my chosen bungalow which, fortunately, was still available.

Moving house is undoubtedly one of life's strange experiences. The day arrives when all your furniture and possessions disappear and you are left with this strange echoing building, quite unrecognisable but filled with familiarity at every turn. You look around and recognise all the blemishes on floors, walls and ceilings; you may even recall the exact event that caused them! You walk around the barren rooms, remembering their functions, remembering all the happy events that took place in them; the bedrooms of your family, the bathroom that always seemed to be occupied, your oh-so-familiar office.

Finally, you tear yourself away and clatter noisily down the stairs to tour the downstairs rooms for the last time, seeing in your mind's eye each room fully furnished, your family lounging in the chairs or squabbling at the table. Then, at last, you force yourself to leave, locking the front door with a totally justified sense of finality. At that moment, you are uprooted and need to be replanted in another place. In my case, I was fortunate enough to be able to replant myself that same day, due to the kindness and cooperation of my buyers and also the sellers of the bungalow.

I still live in this very pleasant bungalow and have been able to convert it to meet the circumstances of my MND.

Meanwhile, I continued my work as the Financial Director of Evans Ltd. Since I had joined the Company in 1996, I had been working hard to achieve the total restructuring and updating of all the administrative and financial practices there. This was achieved single-handedly, since there was no-one else there who had any facility with the modern management and data practices that needed to be applied. It will be recalled that Radclyffe Computer and Management Services had been employed to bring some initial order and efficiency into the company and this led to their offer of employment as Financial Director. In the years leading up to the Millennium, there were great strides forward in technology and this demanded the development of new control programmes and database systems, all controlled by new computer languages.

Now, in 2001, all that reprogramming and updating work was complete – and I became bored! Admittedly, I had managerial responsibilities which stemmed from the frequent absences of the two Managing Directors, who often travelled to Europe and beyond, sourcing the materials they needed for their factory. However, the manufacturing side of the business ran smoothly and was managed at lower levels, while I had set up all the financial, stock control and distribution systems to run automatically under their managers. So, there was no more development work for me to concentrate upon and the day-to-day running of the manufacturing and distribution system ran well without any meaningful input from me. It was at this point that I thought I would retire from the company at the age of fifty-seven. I felt that I had achieved everything I could for Evans. I now felt that I would like to devote my life to helping other people; looking around, I could see that there was a great need for that in the community. Shortly after these thoughts, I met with the Directors to advise them of my plans to retire.

'No, you won't!' This was Carol Evans' testy and dismissive reply. I have to say that such a response was typical of Carol. She was an extremely "plain-speaking" lady who ruled the employees of the company (except me!) with a degree of fear. I was well aware that all the Evans employees approached her with great caution!

In the following robust discussion, it was abundantly clear that neither of my fellow directors wanted me to leave and they pressed me to stay. In the end, I recognised the strength of their feeling and was also gratified to be appreciated so much, so I proposed that I would continue to be the Financial Director of the company for a further three years, that is, until I was sixty. I had always planned to retire when I reached that age. I told them that I would definitely leave the company then and insisted that they should take my words as a full three years notice of my departure!

In fact this did not happen precisely as arranged. As promised, I remained the Financial Director at Evans but, when my 60th birthday approached, I recognised that my departure halfway through the financial year would cause significant difficulty for the company, so in a spirit of fairness I offered to remain in my post until March 2005. This was accepted, I think with some relief, and I completed the financial year while the Directors sought my replacement.

Unfortunately, there are very few accountants who are also computer and data processing specialists! Earlier in this book, I told the story of my ambition and struggle to become a Chartered Accountant. At that time, I had no thoughts of being anything other than an accountant but a developing interest in operating efficiency led me to learning computer programming and data processing techniques, along with an in-depth knowledge of computer hardware. These skills made it possible for me to set up my own computer and management company from which I was "headhunted" by Evans.

Keith and Carol Evans soon found that the sort of specialist they wanted did not seem to be available so they decided to hire two people, an accountant and a computer programmer, to do the job I had done for almost ten years. Two people were recruited and, at the end of the financial year, I duly handed over the appropriate operations and responsibilities to each of them. Within a few months, I learned that the accountant had been discharged as unnecessary and then I was asked if I would come back as a consultant to work just three days a month for a number of months, to return their operating systems to a satisfactory condition. After I had done this, I left Evans (Lichfield) Ltd for a second time and have not returned there since.

During the same period, I was involved in further property operations. I sold my house in Stratford, London (my daughter Helen no longer needed to live there) and decided that I had enjoyed Auckland so very much that I would buy a flat in that city. I travelled once again to New Zealand for a brief two week stay and, with Angela's help, reviewed the housing market there. After a few very busy days of house hunting, I decided to buy a very nice flat in the centre of Auckland and looked forward to living there from time to time. The flat was in a tall, modern building close by the famous Sky Tower. My purchase was on the 10th floor of the building and there were excellent views from all its windows. In addition, the building had a neatly cultivated garden on the roof, where residents could lounge in the sunshine and scan the panoramic view all around.

Although my firm intention was to establish a New Zealand base, I am afraid I never actually lived there! The flat was rented out to various tenants who no doubt enjoyed the views that I had planned for myself. I retained the flat for a number of years (maybe I would actually live there sometime?) but eventually I sold it. Not every plan comes to fruition!

In the first few years of the new millennium, my voluntary responsibilities in the Church increased considerably. First of all, I had been elected a Circuit Steward in 1999. The Circuit Stewards are a small team of three or four people from various churches in the Circuit. Unlike Church Stewards, who support the individual churches where they are members, Circuit Stewards deal with matters relevant to the whole group of churches in the Circuit and are responsible to the Superintendent Minister who oversees the Circuit. I felt greatly honoured to be asked to serve in this capacity.

At the same time, I have to say that being a Circuit Steward is pretty hard work, since there are many responsibilities to fulfil. For instance, the team coordinates all that happens when a minister is replaced in the Circuit; in Methodism, this normally happens every five years. So if the Circuit has five ministers, statistically one will be replaced every year; of course, it never works out like that! There are sometimes two or even three replacements to be dealt with in one year. The procedure involves the relevant churches supplying their "requirements" to the Circuit Stewards who then précis them and pass them on to be published centrally by the Methodist Church. Then, ministers whose appointments will soon terminate review the placements available and apply for the forthcoming vacancies. The Circuit Stewards then have candidates to assess plus visits and interviews to organise. All this generates a considerable amount of work for the team.

In addition, the Circuit Stewards are responsible for the condition of all the manses (minister's houses) in the Circuit. Maintenance and repairs have to be organised. When a minister leaves, the manses have to be prepared for the new minister's arrival. This often involves hard physical work, such as heavy gardening or even scrubbing kitchen floors. I claim to have done many such tasks!

In 2001, I became the Senior Circuit Steward, a position that imposed additional work and responsibilities on me. The Senior Circuit Steward has a leadership role in the team and increased personal responsibilities towards the Superintendent Minister. I was very grateful to have the opportunity of filling this important post for two years. In 2003, my four-year term as a Circuit Steward came to an end and I stepped down from the team.

Almost immediately, I was surprised and greatly flattered to be asked to take on the position of Synod Secretary for the Birmingham District. This is a key position, where one is operating at the Methodist Church "Headquarters" level! Synod is a biannual gathering of all the ministers and officers of the Methodist Church. Twice each year, in Spring and Autumn, Synod meets in different

A Small Piece of Pure Gold

locations across the UK. Obviously, the Synod Secretary has a considerable coordinating and organisational role in every meeting.

I was thrilled and honoured to accept this invitation and this was the start of three very busy years for me, during which I carried out the considerable secretarial and organising work for the six Synods that fell into my stretch. In addition to the Synod, I also had responsibilities towards the organisation of the Methodist Church Conference, a separate and much larger meeting that meets annually and involves all members of the Methodist Church in the UK. Although requiring a great deal of hard work, this was a fascinating time, since it educated me extensively about the highest level of Church politics and administration and brought me into personal contact with most of the current leaders of the Methodist Church in the UK. In particular, I had many dealings with Rev. Bill Anderson, the Chairman of the Birmingham District and we became good friends.

During 2004, Bill Anderson asked me if I would like to spend Christmas with him in the Holy Land. He told me that this was something he had wanted to do for a long time and he would be very pleased if I came along with him to share the experience. I was delighted to accept. This was my first visit to Jerusalem and Bill made sure that we visited all the historical sites, not only in Jerusalem but in the surrounding country, too. It was a truly wonderful experience for me, because we were able to visit many of the places that are mentioned in the Bible. That made the Bible come even more alive for me.

The visit was topped off with an amazing and highly moving experience. On Christmas Eve, we were able to visit the Church of the Nativity in Bethlehem and attend a service there. The church is built on top of a cave called the Grotto. It is here that, traditionally, the birth of Jesus Christ took place. This is, of course, an extremely important site for all branches of Christianity and the church and grotto are administered jointly by the Greek Orthodox, Roman Catholic and Armenian Apostolic Churches.

Services in middle eastern Christian churches are usually much longer than those in the UK. This one lasted five hours and was conducted partly in French and partly in Aramaic. My French is pretty poor but not as poor as my Aramaic – which is non-existent! Of course, Aramaic is thought to be the language that Jesus spoke; it is still spoken in parts of the Middle-East, for instance in some parts of Iran.

For Bill and me, this service was a most incredible experience; listening to the music, drinking in the words even if we could not understand them, participating in the prayers and chants. It was such a privilege to be there. Here we were in the very spot where Jesus had been born all those centuries ago, on the very eve of his birthday. It was a very special and meaningful time which I will never forget. I think that a visit to the Holy Land is an important milestone for all Christians.

It was for this reason that Bill and I decided we should take a party of Birmingham District church people in the following year to see and experience the Holy Land. So in October, 2005, we were once again travelling around the Holy Land, this time guiding our party of Methodists around all the sites that we had enjoyed so much. Everyone had a wonderful and very spiritual time and, for us, it was so good to experience all that amazing Christian history again.

Some months later. after returning to the UK, I met a very charming and inspirational minister from the USA. This was Pastor Jim Tubbs, a Senior Minister of the USA First Christian Church in Pennsylvania. Jim Tubbs was on an evangelical exchange visit with Rev. Bill Anderson. As a friend of Bill, I agreed to "look after" Jim Tubbs while he was on the exchange visit in the UK and resident in Bill Anderson's manse. I was very pleased to spend a good deal of time with him. I showed him around many of the tourist sights of the Midlands region of England and we also visited a number of interesting National Trust properties in the area. I enjoyed his company very much.

When Jim Tubbs was due to return to the USA, he invited me to visit him at his home in Pennsylvania; he would be delighted to "show me around", he said. You may imagine that my "travel bug" leapt within me! I replied that I would be delighted and we arranged that I would contact him in due course.

Once again, it was approaching the time for another Synod to be organised and I set to work with my usual enthusiasm. From my point of view, however, I am afraid that this Synod in September 2006 ended rather unfortunately. Rev. Bill Anderson had been asked to conduct an important service of worship at the end of the Synod with all 150 of the Methodist ministers present. At his instruction, I had prepared a PowerPoint slide presentation to accompany his worship service and would project this for him during the service. The worship was proceeding smoothly until Bill suddenly decided to change the order of a number of elements in his service.

Of course I fully understand that such re-orderings may seem quick and simple to achieve. Unfortunately, in the versions of PowerPoint currently available, such changes cannot be made quickly or easily. I did my best. Even although I am an experienced PowerPoint programmer and operator, I could not meet Bill's requests without disrupting the flow of the service of worship. As a perfectionist in such matters, this left me upset and distinctly agitated. After the relative chaos of this service, I felt unwell, a condition that persisted even after I returned home.

'Nothing that a good night's sleep won't cure,' I thought.

The following day, I awoke with an uncomfortable pain in my chest. As the pain intensified, I remember calling my friend Diane.

'I've got a bad pain in my chest,' I reported to her.

Diane's advice to me was immediate and uncompromising. 'Call the doctor,' she said.

I demurred. I don't like to make a fuss! 'Can you come round?' This was my response. I always depended on my wonderful friend Diane!

Diane soon appeared, took one look at me and called the doctor. The doctor spoke to me and asked about my symptoms, then immediately instructed that we should call "999" for an ambulance. The emergency crew arrived with impressive speed and transported me to hospital, where the medical assessment suggested strongly that I was experiencing a heart attack.

Like so many others who arrive at the Accident and Emergency (A&E) Department of a hospital, I then spent many hours lying uncomfortably on a trolley. I was informed that a bed would become available in the Cardiac Unit in "due course". My very long wait in A&E was far from a pleasant experience but, when you have had a heart attack, you are very grateful to be in the hands of medical emergency experts and would certainly not choose to be elsewhere.

Eventually, I was taken to the Cardiac Unit, which was much more comfortable. I was informed that I would undergo a procedure called an "angiogram" to establish the problem in my heart. In a procedure carried out under local anaesthetic, the angiogram passes a carbon fibre camera system through an artery to the heart and establishes the location and nature of the problem. In a heart attack situation, a blockage or severe narrowing of one or more arteries will be found.

After the angiogram was completed, I was informed that a heart attack had been confirmed and I would now undergo an operation to correct the problems found. This operation, an angioplasty, inserts one or more "stents" into the artery to clear the blockage and restore the artery so that normal blood flow will be re-established. For this operation, I needed to be transferred to a larger hospital in Birmingham and the procedure, again under local anaesthetic, was successful, with two stents inserted into arteries of my heart.

Thereafter, an excellent régime of rehabilitation was offered at my local hospital where medically supervised exercises built up my fitness. At the end of the program, I was advised I should maintain my fitness by attending a local "Heartcare" gym, where there were professional and medical staff members who would continue to advise and monitor me.

Knowing that my friend Jack (who is writing this book!) was attending this gym after a rather similar cardiac experience several years before, I contacted him and he took me to the gym and introduced me to the staff there. Thereafter, we both attended the gym regularly twice a week and did so for many years.

Of course, it was necessary for me to resign from my position as Synod Secretary.

Today (Summer 2015) I still visit the Heartcare gym and have many friends there. However, the progression of my MND means that I am no longer able to participate in any of the exercise regimes.

15

Nearly A Road Too Far

Two years earlier in 2004, while I was Synod Secretary, I was asked if I would consider becoming the Treasurer of the Birmingham City Mission, a long-established initiative that had been set up in Birmingham during the 19th Century. Its headquarters and offices were in the Methodist Central Hall, located in the middle of Birmingham. Of course the Mission had come into being at a time of great poverty and deprivation in the City and it operated to alleviate suffering and educate people in the Christian way. Obviously, as time passed, Mission operations were altered to meet the problems of the day. Today, the Mission owns a range of shops in Birmingham and the rentals from these premises provide substantial funds for its continuing charity work. I reviewed the work of the Treasurer and decided that it was within my capacity to help.

Thus, I joined the Committee of eight members (ministers and lay people) and soon discovered that none of them had any direct experience of modern financial operations. I also found that the Mission's financial structures were greatly outdated. In consequence, I set to work immediately to modernise these. This meant that I had to restructure various internal financial procedures and I soon found that my Committee colleagues were reluctant to adopt change. Over the years that I served as Treasurer, I did my best (with some success) to persuade them that modern accounting procedures were necessary for the health and efficiency of the Mission.

During my review of the operations, I noted that a particular function of the Mission had been a continuous and long-lasting drain on finances. This was the "Law Courts Family Centre", a welfare initiative that had been set up in the early days of the Mission to solve a serious problem of the day. The Mission was located just across the street from the Birmingham Law Courts and it had been noted that, when the citizens of Birmingham were required to answer a summons to the Courts, their children were left outside, totally abandoned; children were not, of course, allowed into the hallowed premises of the Law Courts. Left alone, unattended and unguarded, the children were prey to a whole range of serious dangers. The Mission determined to set up a Family Centre where the children could be deposited and kept safely until their parents returned to collect them.

When I became Treasurer, the Family Centre was still in operation with a full-time staff. However, the social conditions of the 21st Century meant that very few children now attended – on some days, the records showed that there had been just one young child looked after for a few hours during a whole day. After reviewing the situation and its costs, I proposed to the Committee that the Family Centre was very uneconomical to operate and recommended that it should be closed down. My Committee colleagues demurred but eventually decided that the situation should be reviewed by independent experts. Eventually, an external report recommended closure and the unused Family Centre was eventually closed.

My tenure as Birmingham City Mission Treasurer was to end in 2009.

Now that I was free from my duties as Synod Secretary and in better health, I decided that in 2007 I should be off on my travels once again. I would visit New Zealand at Christmastime – Christmas celebrations in mid-summer are splendid! However, this time, I planned to make this into more of a round-the-world trip by firstly flying to the USA to take up the kind invitation of my friend Jim Tubbs, who you will remember was the American minister who came to the UK on an exchange visit with Rev. Bill Anderson, the Birmingham District Chairman.

Jim Tubbs welcomed me cordially into his home and introduced me to his friends and family. I greatly enjoyed visiting his church and was most pleased to worship with his very enthusiastic congregations. Just as I had shown him around the sights of England (a few of them, anyway!), Jim Tubbs took me to many interesting places, showing me all around the Pittsburgh, Pennsylvania area, where I remember visiting museums and a particularly inspiring exhibition of wonderful glassware.

He then asked me if I had ever been to Niagara Falls. When I said I had not, he announced his intention of taking me there. 'This is a sight that everyone should see during their lifetime,' he said.

Jim was right. We went to see the Canadian Falls, which are the largest and most spectacular of the three named waterfalls in the area. To do this, we had to take our passports with us so that we could cross the frontier into Canada. From whatever angle you view Horseshoe Falls, they are a truly awesome sight. From a distance, their sheer scale is awesome and the roaring of vast quantities of foaming, rushing water creates a continuous and distinctive noise, day and night. An extensive viewing area is built close to the point where the bright green water tumbles over the edge and plunges down almost 200 feet to the river below. Here, one is almost deafened by the volume of the noise and stunned by the pure quantity of the water flow, said to be around 100,000 cubic feet per second!

At the base of the huge waterfall, a thick curtain of mist rises, into which the sturdy tourist boats (all named "Maid of the Mist 1,2,3" etc.) power their way towards the huge curtain of plummeting water, thrusting against the racing, boiling water on maximum engine power to give the tourists on board an unparalleled view of millions of tons of water falling directly in front of them. After a few stationary moments, the boats cut their power, and veer away sharply to be swept away at high speed until they regain the somewhat calmer waters some way downstream. There are also caves behind the Horseshoe Falls, where it is possible to stand on open viewing platforms only feet away from the dense curtain of water racing past. All this is an astounding experience.

Subsequently, Jim took me to Washington DC – a long journey south from his home. Here, we checked into a very pleasant hotel near the Capitol, the centre of Government in the USA. We then spent the following days visiting the sights of Washington. It was logical to start with the Capitol building, a dramatic, pure white building with a large dome, built over 200 years ago on the top of historic Capitol Hill. There are extensive tours throughout the building and we took full advantage of them, spending several very enjoyable hours there.

From the impressive and dominating frontage of the Capitol, the National Mall stretches westwards as two wide pedestrian walkways with a stretch of grass in between, leading first to the Washington Memorial, a very famous tall white obelisk constructed of marble and granite. The National Mall then continues westwards, with the centre grass strip replaced by a lengthy "Reflecting Pool", which displays excellent inverted images of both the Lincoln and the Washington Memorials, depending upon the observer's viewpoint.

The western end of the Mall then terminates in the dominating and extremely impressive Lincoln Memorial, a large rectangular building built in the style of a Doric temple. After mounting the many wide steps at the front at the front of the building, we entered between the towering columns to stand gazing in awe at the gigantic and very famous statue of a seated Abraham Lincoln, 16th President of the United States of America. Serving as President during 1861 to 1865, Abraham Lincoln led his country successfully though the American Civil War, preserved the Union and set the Country on a truly modern course.

Not very far north of the Washington Memorial obelisk is the White House, famously at the address 1600 Pennsylvania Avenue. This is another magnet for tourists and we were able to obtain tickets from a booth nearby which would allow us to join a White House tour at a specific time later that day. I was a little surprised to find that the tickets were completely free; this is part of the American philosophy – the White House belongs to all citizens and it is therefore inappropriate to charge any fee!

Again, this was a wonderfully interesting visit. We were guided around all parts of the White House apart from the President's private accommodation, of course. All the state and government rooms were visited, including the very famous "Oval Office", seen on film and television many times. Afterwards, we were able to stroll freely around the White House gardens, too.

I enjoyed Jim Tubb's company so very much and I was deeply grateful to him for spending so much time (and money) on me. Now it was time for me to start on the next part of my "world tour" which would end up in New Zealand at Christmastime. From Philadelphia, I had planned to take an internal flight to Vancouver, located on Canada's west coast, just north of the northern border of the USA. I had thought that I might take advantage of a tour to the Canadian Rockies (many people had told me what a wonderful experience this is), but now I realised that I had only six days before my flight left for New Zealand. This, I concluded, was certainly not long enough to undertake a visit to the Rockies. Accordingly, I decided I would re-plan for these six days and tour around Vancouver Island, a very large, rugged island just off the coast of this part of Canada. I would hire a rental car, book a few hotels at various places on the island and tour around, relaxing and enjoying myself. Then I would return to Vancouver in good time for my flight to New Zealand.

Vancouver Island is part of the Canadian state of British Columbia. The island is of considerable size, extending to 300 miles in length and 50 miles wide at its widest point. Somewhat surprisingly, Vancouver, the largest city of British Columbia is not the state capital; instead, it is Victoria, a much smaller and less populous city located at the southern tip of Vancouver Island. The reason is, apparently, rooted in 19th Century Canadian politics.

Around three-quarters of a million people live on Vancouver Island; apart from Victoria, which is the largest population centre, there are five more cities or large towns and many other smaller centres of population. Unsurprisingly, most habitations are situated on the sheltered eastern side of the island; western areas present rugged and barren coasts to the rigours of the Pacific Ocean. The middle of the island is distinctly mountainous, with snow-capped peaks that rise to over 7,000 feet. I was surprised to learn that there are several glaciers in these mountains, the largest of which is the Comox Glacier.

After I had completed all the necessary research on Vancouver Island, I rented a modest ("Compact") car and made one-night hotel reservations at four different locations on Vancouver Island, one of which was in the town of Tofino, situated on the very rugged western coast. This, I reasoned, would offer me experience not only of the remote and exposed western coast but give me a taste of the bleak, uninhabited inland parts of the island too. Finally, I made the necessary investigations about car ferries, since a number of routes link Vancouver Island with the mainland. I would travel out on a southerly ferry to Victoria but would return on one of the crossings further north. Now I was all set to start my next adventure!

I had no problems on the first or second days. The pleasant ferry crossing took several hours and, after checking into my hotel in Victoria, I was able to explore some of the city and its surroundings and take in a few tourist attractions. The next morning, I started on my northward journey. The roads were good but very busy, especially in the south near Victoria and its suburbs. Route 1 starts in Victoria and runs north as a wide, divided roadway. After a time, Route 1 becomes Route 19 and this major road continues north on the eastern side of the Island (but not always near the coast) until it reaches Port Hardy, hundreds of miles away in the far northeast of the island.

However, my journey today was to take me to Parksville, where I had booked accommodation in a hotel. Parksville is a sprawling town built around a large sandy beach on the east coast, over 100 miles north of Victoria. With its beaches, extensive parks and sports facilities, as well as opportunities to observe many species of wildlife, it is a holiday destination set up for a large range of outdoor activities. I arrived there in mid-afternoon and spent the rest of the day strolling around and generally relaxing.

On the third day, I was scheduled to make my way to the rugged western coast of the island, to the town of Tofino. Highway 4 begins at Parksville and leads across the mountains to the western coast. Then it turns north and terminates in the remote town of Tofino. I was fascinated

A Small Piece of Pure Gold

to see what this remote town would be like. This was to be a day of adventure and I looked forward to it eagerly.

As I drove out of Parksville on Highway 4A, I reflected what a nice wide, smooth road it was, every bit as good as Highway 19. However, I was aware that Highway 4A would soon become Highway 4 and, looking on the map, I could see that this became very much of a mountain road, showing many sweeps and turns as it negotiated the contours of the land. After a few miles, I turned left on to Highway 4 and I could see immediately that this was a different standard of road – much narrower and not a dual carriageway.

Traffic was much lighter on Highway 4 as I drove at moderate speed along the road which twisted and turned around the increasingly undulating ground contours. Much of the land on each side of the road was thickly wooded with conifer trees so, to my disappointment, the drama of the countryside was often hidden from view. As my journey progressed, I could see that the road was becoming significantly more undulating and I observed high mountains looming ahead. Of course I was climbing directly towards this area of mountains. For quite a long time, the road ran on the northern side of a long lake. I'm sure the views would have been beautiful but, again, tall conifer trees on each side of the road continued to obscure the view almost completely.

Soon, there were steeper climbs to negotiate and traffic became much more sparse. The road was increasingly precipitous, set along the edge of steep slopes. Looking up, I could see that the mountains ahead were deeply snow-covered.

'Well', I thought to myself, 'why not? It's winter, isn't it? And we all know that Vancouver Island is cold enough to have glaciers in its mountains!'

Of course Highway 4 did not head for the mountain peaks but wound around them at lower elevations; nevertheless, I could see that the road ahead was still rising steeply. Quite suddenly, there was deep snow on each side although the road surface was still clear.

'Swept clean by the traffic or maybe the odd snow plough,' I thought, with a faint smile. As I continued, it occurred to me that I seemed to be the only vehicle venturing on this road.

Then, quite suddenly, my tyres were crunching through several inches of snow on the road. Clearly, the temperature outside was well below freezing and the snow was icy and crystalline in nature. The road in this higher ground area was cut into very steep, wooded slopes, soaring to thousands of feet on the left and plunging down on the right – the side of the road on which I was travelling.

I am (like all men!) a highly experienced driver who, over the years, has driven many cars in snow and icy conditions. I assessed the situation carefully and decided that there was little danger. I had already slowed right down but I knew I should keep moving. If I stopped I may not have sufficient grip to start moving again, I thought. At present, this current section of road was largely flat and the next bend was some distance away. I noted that there were no retaining barriers at the road edge; earlier, I had seen retaining barriers on the road but it seems that they were installed only at bends.

Behind the wheel, I relaxed. 'There's no danger here,' I told myself, 'If I just maintain my very modest speed and keep going smoothly, I will be fine.'

Suddenly, alarmingly, the car started to drift offline towards the road edge and I felt the steering wheel become very light in my hands.

'Ice below the snow,' I muttered grimly. 'That's unfortunate!'

I tried to correct the drift by steering the car gently to the left but the front tyres failed to have any grip on the ice. The car totally ignored my attempt to control its direction and continued its slither towards the edge of the road. I felt a pang of concern, rapidly turning to worry. I knew I needed to act quickly! I had to stop the car before it was completely out of control! It was then that I tried to brake, to reduce speed and bring the car to a stop, but this had absolutely no retarding effect. The car merely turned into a very efficient sledge and appeared to accelerate down the road camber at the edge of the ice-covered asphalt.

The next moments became a surreal version of slow motion. As I continued to wrestle with apparently disconnected controls, the car left the smooth road surface and, gathering pace, slithered across the few feet of frozen, ice-covered ballast at the roadside before launching itself resolutely over the unprotected, precipitous edge. This was followed almost immediately by a colossal shock as the car impacted deafeningly on the steeply-angled snow-covered slope below, first the front end and then the back. Without pause, gravity and momentum joined forces to accelerate the car down the mountain's precipitous and terrifying snow-covered slope.

It has been said many times that, in such circumstances, your life flashes before you. Mine didn't! Instead, I was frozen in disbelief that such a thing could be happening but I was beginning to realise that I would soon be travelling at considerable speed, totally out of control and waiting despairingly for a collision that would either injure me grievously or terminate my life. At that instant, I recognised that the car was heading squarely for a large stout conifer tree not far down the slope.

The impact was petrifying. The noise was unbelievable. The front of the car bludgeoned its way through the lower branches of the tree and crumpled itself (as it was designed to do) against the unyielding, solid trunk within. The radiator was breached and huge jets of boiling water and steam jetted into the air. Inside the car, copious quantities of noxious fumes surged out from various vents. The air bags, a primary source of safety in a modern car, failed to deploy but I was held firmly in my seat by an automatically tightened seat belt.

I suppose I sat there for a few seconds as the worst of the noise and commotion died away to a sullen silence relieved only by the creaking and susurration of rapidly cooling metal, plastic and liquids. I forced my mind to monitor my body's internal and external functions as best as I could and concluded that, miraculously, I might be uninjured – and saved! In any event, I thought, sitting in a smashed car that must be in danger of catching fire was clearly a hazardous thing to do, so, carefully, I released my seatbelt, opened the door (fortunately, it was not jammed) and climbed out very gingerly, testing the operation of each limb carefully before I used it.

Beside the wrecked car, I stood still. Physically, I thought I was probably uninjured. I could not feel any pain and everything seemed to be working with some semblance of normality. Of course I was shocked and not a little disorientated. The silence of the mountain was restored and, for an unknown time, total unreality sealed me in a viscous cocoon of inaction. Eventually, I thought: 'What should I do?' It was very difficult to think, to decide. I don't know how long I stood there, looking blankly at the smashed car but, eventually, I forced my limbs to move, scrambled up the steep slope through the snow and, with agonising difficulty, managed to drag myself on to the road level above. It was freezing. I was shivering uncontrollably. But I was alive. Definitely.

Some time later (maybe half an hour?) the noise of an engine heralded the approach of a vehicle, travelling slowly in the same direction I had been. It proved to be a small car. I stood out in the road and waved at the driver to stop. As it came close, I saw that a solitary lady was driving the car. She stopped beside me, lowered her window and asked me what was wrong.

'I've had an accident,' I told her. 'My car skidded on the ice and ran off the road. It's down there.' I pointed down the slope.

'Are you all right?' the woman asked.

A Small Piece of Pure Gold

'Well, yes, I think so,' I answered. 'Do you think you could you give me a lift to Tofino?'

The woman looked doubtful. 'OK,' she said finally, 'get in'.

'Can I just get my bag from the car?' I asked, pointing down the slope.

'No!' the woman responded and immediately drove off!

I didn't (and I don't) blame this woman, although her abandonment could have had serious consequences for me. Obviously, the presence of a strange man on a mountain road in the middle of winter proved too much for her and she became terrified at the prospect of my presence alone with her in the car.

It was probably another half hour before another vehicle arrived, this time (very much to my relief), it was a man.

'Where is it?' he asked in puzzlement when I told him about my accident, 'I can't see any car.'

It was true. Even from the roadside, the car was practically invisible as it was now partially embedded in a large conifer tree. I had to direct the man's gaze to the rear of the car before he was able to discern its position.

'Come on,' he said, I'll help you get your bag and anything else you need from the car.' We both slid our way down and were soon back with my belongings.

The man said he was pleased to help me and give me a lift to Tofino. 'That's where I'm going,' he told me. 'I'll record the number of kilometres we travel so that you'll know where the car is. Otherwise, you may never be able to find it again.' I thought that was an excellent idea and congratulated him.

Although this day appeared to be of infinite length, it was not yet midday when we arrived in Tofino. I thanked the man profusely when he dropped me off at my hotel.

'Glad to help,' he replied, 'I hope everything goes OK with you. Here's the distance we've travelled from your accident,' he said, giving me a piece of paper with the number of kilometres noted on it.

The rest of the day was filled with the consequences of the accident. I spent a long time on the telephone, informing the car hire company in Vancouver about the accident. They replied that they would send a breakdown truck to pick up the wrecked car. The breakdown vehicle would bring a replacement car for me, they said. They also told me that I must report the accident to the police in Tofino because they would need an accident report for the insurers. I went to the Police Station and told my story. Inevitably, it took a long time to compile the report. However, it was clear that the police were not interested in what had happened, since it had been a single vehicle accident and no one had been injured. Nevertheless. there had to be a plethora of paperwork with much for me to sign!

Tofino is a small town with less than 2000 residents. Originally a small fur trading post, it became a centre for logging when a rudimentary road was driven through the mountains. This road, (the one I had just experienced!) was not paved until the 1970s. However, Tofino has long been a tourist destination for Canadians, even in the mid-19th Century, with the wild and beautiful countryside encouraging a whole range of outdoor land and sea activities. In the rather restricted free time that I had, I was able to have a little walkabout the town and sample a little of the ambiance of the place.

It was ten o'clock that evening when the car hire mechanic arrived in his breakdown truck, towing a worryingly identical car on a trailer rig behind the truck! I went to meet the driver and identified myself.

'Didn't see it,' he said laconically as he shook my hand. 'Kept looking all the way. Got to take it back to Vancouver, you know. How do I find it?'

A Small Piece of Pure Gold

I sighed. I knew what I had to do! 'I think I can find it for you,' I said wearily, 'I know how many kilometres along the road it is. I'll come back with you, if you want.'

'OK,' the mechanic said, 'we'll leave right away. We'll keep the replacement car attached to the truck as ballast.' He climbed into the truck. 'Let's go.' I climbed stiffly into the truck.

It was midnight when we had travelled the number of kilometres written on the card. Of course it was pitch dark and everything looks different in the dark! 'Stop here,' I told the mechanic, 'I'm sure it's on this stretch of road.' I kept saying this, as we trampled up and down, shining a powerful torch beam down the slope. Eventually, after quite some time, we managed to locate the car.

'Right,' the mechanic said, 'I'll unhitch the replacement car and then winch the other one up to the road.' The mechanic had obviously carried out this sort of operation many times and, before long, he was winching the smashed vehicle up to the road. (I have a short video sequence of the car, tilted at 45 degrees, being inched up to road level.) Once there, the mechanic soon had the wrecked car installed on his trailer rig behind the breakdown truck.

'OK, I've got to get back to Vancouver,' he said briskly to me, 'It'll take me the rest of the night, so I had better get going. Here are the keys for your replacement car. You're going back to Tofino, aren't you? Anyway,' he concluded perfunctorily, 'all the best to you, I hope you make it OK! Got to get going.' As he said this he swung into his cab, fired up the engine and drove off.

I watched the tail lights of the vehicle diminish and disappear around a bend in the road before I looked ruefully at my "new" car. You may imagine that I regarded the prospect of driving back to Tofino with some dismay! For some moments, I stood, completely alone once again on this deserted road where so much had happened to me. However, there was nothing for it, now I had so step into this eerily identical car and drive along the same icy road that had almost killed me! I did so – very cautiously, not exceeding walking pace! Fortunately, the road began to descend (I was grateful that the slope was very gentle) and the snow and ice soon diminished and cleared. The rest of the drive to Tofino, while not very pleasant in the pitch darkness, was without incident. The Lord be praised!

The next day, after only a few hours of sleep, I had to leave Tofino and drive back along the same mountain road, through the snow and ice once again, since my next stop was back on the eastern coast! I did it, successfully and very carefully!

My next hotel was in Campbell River on the east coast of the island, about 80 miles north of Parksville, so I had to undertake quite a long drive on that day. After the mountain roads, driving on the east coast Highway 19 was very pleasant and traffic became somewhat lighter the further north you travelled. In due course, I completed my journey to Campbell River and checked into my hotel.

After a short rest, I then decided to go for a walk, to clear my head after all the excitement I had been through. This did not quite go to plan however! I enjoyed walking several miles northwards along a stony beach and then, because the beach had become rather uncomfortable to walk upon, decided to strike inland and walk back along a road to the town. After a while, I suddenly realised I was lost!

'This is ridiculous!' I thought, yet I could not decide in which direction I should head. Finally, in some despair, I spotted a lone house in the distance away and decided to seek advice there.

'I hope someone is at home,' I thought as I approached the house. There was! A man opened the door and I explained my predicament to him. I think he took one look at me and said:

'Just a minute. I'll just get my car out of the garage and I'll run you back to town.'

A Small Piece of Pure Gold

I was most grateful to this man for his kindness and I greatly appreciated not having to walk all the way back. I made sure that I noted his name and address and subsequently wrote to thank him.

The following day, my somewhat ill-fated tour of Vancouver Island was coming to an end and I hoped that there would be no further dramas as I used a different ferry to cross the Strait and return to Vancouver City. Within a couple of days, I was due to start my journey to New Zealand and, I must say, I looked forward to a bit of tranquil relaxation!

The flight to New Zealand was uneventful and I had a very pleasant Christmas with Angela and her friends. During the weeks I was there, I took the opportunity of visiting many other friends on both North and South Islands. For me, travel is not just about "seeing the sights", beautiful and awesome though many of these are, it is also about meeting old friends and making new ones. The God-given gifts of love, friendship and fellowship are certainly one of the most important facets of human life.

16

God's Amazing People

My travels in 2008 were by no means over yet, because now I planned to return home via Australia and South Africa. I have always found that I learn a great deal from my travels, not because I see and experience vast tracts of strange lands (although it is remarkable how physically varied the world is) but because of what I learn from the people I meet. In other words, my itineraries tend to be a series of people rather than places.

In Melbourne, Australia, it was wonderful to meet up again with my friend John Pernu. Formerly a minister, John now had a small business of his own and seemed to be happy and well-established. I also determined to visit the daughter of a dear friend of mine back in Sutton Coldfield. The internal flight from Melbourne to Sydney was uneventful and I spent a very enjoyable time with the family there, seeing the many sights of that great city before I returned to Melbourne.

Subsequently, I flew to the city of Perth on the western coast of Austria (seemed a pity to fly over it and not visit!) and then on to South Africa to join a 25-day tour that would take me around many parts of this beautiful and amazing country.

My rail journey from Melbourne City to the airport where I would board my plane to Perth proved more hectic than expected. Having purchased my ticket, I asked to be directed to the platform from which my train would leave. Having arrived at that platform, I checked with a railway official that the train already standing there was going to the airport. It was and I was directed to board it. Shortly afterwards the train left the station.

As I sat back and relaxed on the seat cushions, watching the scenery go by, it gradually dawned upon me that I was travelling in the opposite direction I wanted to go! It is an uniquely disquieting experience to realise that, instead of making progress towards your objective, you are being borne further away – at an ever-increasing speed – and there isn't a single thing you can do about it. You are totally powerless and it is a truly horrible feeling as you realise you might miss your flight! You just have to sit there, far from relaxed, hoping that the train's first stop isn't going to be 100 miles away!

After what seemed an age, the train slowed and stopped at its first station, fortunately not too many miles away from my departure point. I stepped off gratefully and started the process of finding the way back to my starting point. At the second attempt, I did manage to arrive at the airport and was happy to note that I still had sufficient time to check-in and board my flight.

My flight touched down at Johannesburg Airport, from where I transferred to the capital city of Pretoria, some 40 miles away. I soon met up with the other members of the tour at the hotel where we were staying the night. During the following 24 days, we travelled very extensively around South Africa, penetrating also into the southern part of Mozambique for a time and also traversing several land-locked states such as Swaziland and Lesotho. We visited the very famous Kruger National Park as well as a number of other National Parks and Game Reserves.

There was a multiplicity of spectacular sights to be seen, dramatic mountainous regions, precipitous cliffs, magnificent lakes, rivers and waterfalls.

The coastal cities of Durban and Port Elizabeth were two of several coastal stops and the tour eventually terminated in Cape Town. Here, a cable car ride to the top of Table Mountain gave panoramic views for hundreds of miles around and a visit to Robben Island provided a sobering visit to the prison accommodation of the legendary Nelson Mandela. There was also a very welcome visit to Stellenbosch, centre of a principal wine-growing area of South Africa, where it was possible (and encouraged) to sample the excellent wines produced there!

However, it was the human contrasts that struck me most. Apartheid may be long gone in the country but it seemed to me that there was still a huge variation in the lifestyles of the white and black inhabitants. While the former were generally affluent (some extremely rich), huge numbers of the black population live in relative poverty. Every large city we visited had extensive slum areas occupied by many thousands of black families.

When our tour took us into southern Mozambique, the poverty was even more horrifying. Our tour guides warned us about beggars and the general advice was to have as little contact as possible with the local population. Most of my fellow tourists took this advice and tended to huddle together. However, that is not my way! I think that personal contact with the people of other countries teaches one so much.

Our coach had stopped for a break in a small town square in Mozambique. There were many tumbledown slum dwellings to be seen but, inevitably, one side of the square had a long row of large, smart dwellings – obviously, this was where the "rich" people lived. As usual, our group huddled around the coach and generally ignored the local people. Looking around, I observed a boy, a young teenager, sitting silently on a low wall not far away. I strolled across and sat on the wall beside him, greeting him with a smile and engaging him in conversation. He looked at me silently as I talked. Eventually, without looking at me, he spoke very quietly.

'I really must get a job,' he said. 'I have no money.'

I paused for a moment or two. 'Listen,' I said, looking straight into his face to be sure I had his attention, 'you see these rich houses over there?'

He looked across the square and then returned his gaze to me, wordlessly. 'Go over there,' I continued, 'knock on every one of these doors and ask them for a job.' He didn't move. 'Go and do it now,' I insisted.

I watched him as he walked slowly across the square and began knocking at the house doors. I saw him have a brief conversation with whoever opened the doors. Then he moved along to the next door and repeated the process. I watched him approach every one of these houses.

I hoped that he would get a positive response from at least one of the houses he approached. I prayed that he would but, as far as I could see from my viewpoint, I don't think he did. But the important point was, he was actively trying! My words to him had been successful in galvanising him into action and now I hoped and prayed that, having taken his courage in both hands on this first occasion, he would be motivated to keep up the pressure to succeed. Life is like that. Success often does not come easily; it requires hard and sustained work and effort. I think of this boy today and I send my blessings to him for his success in life.

I have already mentioned the great contrasts in living conditions across the whole area and this brings another vivid occasion to mind. On this occasion, the tour had stopped on a gigantic farm where a number of tourist cabins had been built. While the tourist party confined themselves to the nearest bar and restaurant, I went exploring!

I could see an imposing mansion in the distance, which was obviously the residence of the landowner. I followed the road that led to this very large house, eventually arriving at tall railings with large ornamental gates set within them. The wide road continued through the gates and led up to the residence, looking even more magnificent on closer inspection. I saw that there was a small white child playing on a bicycle in front of the house and, as I looked, a man came out of the front door. Seeing me standing at the gate, he walked across and I introduced myself and told him I was one of the tourists living overnight in one of his cabins.

'You have a very beautiful house here,' I said to him, 'have you lived here for long?'

The man was friendly. 'Yes, I've lived here for ages. This is my brother's house. He is the landowner here. He's off on holiday at the moment. Gone fishing in New Zealand.'

'That's a coincidence,' I said, 'I've just come from New Zealand, via Australia.'

We had a pleasant chat for a while and then I took my leave. As I looked around, I saw in the distance what looked like a huge mound of rubbish, a veritable mountain of scrap and waste of all kinds. Ever curious, I decided that I would have to investigate. It was a fair walk to this huge mound and, as I approached it, I confirmed my original opinion – it was a huge quantity of all sorts of rubbish from farm and household. I wondered how they dealt with this situation – surely it must be cleared or reduced from time to time.

It was then that I became aware of a tall, well-made black man standing silently some distance away, watching me expressionlessly. I immediately approached him and told him who I was. 'Just out for a walk after sitting on a coach for so long,' I explained. 'Are you a worker on this estate?'

'Yes, Sir,' he said, 'I am the man who looks after this area. I am responsible for it.'

I looked up at the huge dump of rubbish. 'How do you look after it,' I asked.

'I keep it as tidy as I can,' he said. 'It is my job.'

'Do you work for the man who owns this estate?'

'Yes, Sir, I do.'

'Where do you live?' I said, looking around for some worker's houses. There was nothing to be seen anywhere.

'I live here,' the man said, 'with my family.'

'Here?' I asked in puzzlement.

'Yes, Sir. Come, I'll show you.'

We walked around the huge rubbish dump and headed for a rusty, battered freight container – the sort you see being lifted on and off ships. 'I live here with my family,' the man said, indicating the container.

I was astonished. It was obvious that the owner of this estate and his family lived in great luxury, in a large house with extensive, beautiful grounds. Yet here was his employee, carrying out what looked like a very unpleasant job, given only an old freight container to live in, situated beside this evil-smelling rubbish dump. 'Apartheid,' I thought, 'it's supposed to be gone. But this looks like apartheid to me.'

There was a young boy standing nearby, obviously one of the man's children. 'What about your son here,' I asked, pointing to the boy, 'does he go to school?'

The man looked sad. 'No,' he said, 'I wish he did go to school but I cannot afford to pay. The Master here does not pay me much money. Everything I receive we need to spend on food and essential clothes. We never have anything left.'

Again, I was shocked and deeply touched. 'I want to give you this for your family,' I said, giving him all the money I had in my pocket. 'it is to help you and your family and to send your children to school.'

Some days later in the tour, our coach had stopped at a village and we were encouraged to visit a row of local market stalls which had been set up nearby. We were told that this was the local market in this village and the traders were keen that we should come and view the range of excellent local goods they had for sale. Clearly, it was an enterprise aimed at tourists and, no doubt for a suitable fee from the traders, the tour guides would bring a succession of coaches to this place.

So I started at the first stall and examined the range of goods on sale, eventually buying a few souvenirs. I did the same at the second stall and finally exhausted the money I was carrying at the third stall. There were still a number of other stalls to examine and I came to one where the stallholder was a lone woman, standing quietly beside the small quantity of goods she was offering for sale.

'Please buy something from my stall,' she said to me quietly, 'I have many good things to sell.'

'I am afraid, I cannot buy anything,' I responded. 'I've spent all my money at the other stalls up there.' I pointed to the beginning of the row of stalls.

The woman looked very disappointed and downcast, not sure whether to believe me.

'It's true,' I said, 'I really have no money in my pockets. I spent it all up there.'

She seemed to be a very pleasant woman and I asked her about her business with the stall.

'I have lost my husband so I must work to bring up my children,' she told me. 'When I was left alone, I was desperate to earn money. Although most stallholders are men, I decided to set up a stall here. It was not easy to do but by persistence I succeeded. I persuaded some friends to make me a stall and then I went to spend all I had to buy goods to sell. And now I can make some money every day to look after my children and send them to school.'

I was greatly impressed by this brave woman. 'Listen,' I said, 'you should not set up your stall here, you should set it up at the beginning of the row, up there.' I pointed, 'because that's where most of the tourist money is spent.'

A Small Piece of Pure Gold

In saying this, I was aware that the stallholders may not be free to set up where they like – that is certainly what happens with market stalls in UK – but, even if that is the case, perhaps the woman can apply for a better pitch than she had at the moment.

As I spoke, I decided that I wanted to help this woman and her family. She had been left alone by the death of her husband and with the responsibility of children to bring up. She seemed to be doing this successfully without help from anyone, using a combination of courage and hard work. I determined to help her.

'Give me your name and address,' I said, 'I would like to help you and your family. I will send you some money when I return to the UK.'

The woman thanked me and supplied her name and address, probably thinking that she was unlikely to hear from me ever again! She was wrong! I did send her some money as I had promised and she responded with a very grateful letter of thanks, telling me how my money was helping her family to progress. I responded to this by sending her some more money.

However, I know that giving people money is not always the answer but this woman's story, at that small market stall in a remote part of Southern Africa, touched my heart and I know that God wanted me respond in that way. By contrast, in another part of the country, I was approached by a beggar woman in a food market. She was claiming that her family was poor and very hungry. I turned to a nearby stall and asked the woman if she would like me to buy her a generous bunch of beautiful, ripe bananas. She said she would like to have the bananas, so I bought them from the stallholder and handed them to her.

'You must give me money also,' the woman said, holding out her hand, 'my family is poor and starving and this is not enough for them.'

'No,' I said, 'I asked you if you wanted these bananas and you said yes. I have bought these for you and I hope that you and your family will enjoy them. I am giving you nothing more but God bless you.'

I had the impression that she was not at all pleased!

Sometimes, it is right to give money. Sometimes it isn't!

About halfway through our tour, we arrived in the large city of Durban, on the east coast of South Africa. Our coach dropped us at our hotel. When I had settled into my room, I wanted to send some emails (I always like to keep in touch with my friends worldwide!) and enquired at the Reception Desk about a Wi-Fi connection to my room. To my surprise, I was advised that there were absolutely no Wi-Fi connections available in the hotel.

'OK,' I said, 'where is the nearest internet café? I will just go there.'

The receptionist was horrified! 'No, Sir! You must not do that. You cannot go outside alone. You will be robbed.' This advice was reinforced by the Manager who had overheard the conversation: 'It is very dangerous to walk in the street alone. Many foreigners have been robbed. They have been injured, even killed! You must not go outside on your own!'

I thanked the hotel staff for their advice and decided to ignore it! After all, it was still daylight outside and there was nothing sinister to be seen; the street outside was quiet, calm and normal. If there were no Wi-Fi connections in the hotels, there must be an internet café nearby, I reasoned. I would find out where one was and stroll along, send my emails and stroll back to the hotel in time for dinner.

'I've certainly been in more dangerous places than this,' I thought.

So I donned my backpack (just to identify myself positively as a foreign tourist!) and left the hotel. There was plenty of traffic on the road but few pedestrians as I strolled along, scanning the shops to locate an internet café. After a while, I saw a lone young black man walking towards me.

'Excuse me,' I said as he came close, 'could you direct me to an internet café?'

The young man looked at me with some puzzlement. 'You want an internet café?' he asked.

'Yes, I have some emails I want to send.'

He looked worried and concerned and looked around nervously. 'OK,' he said finally, 'I can show you. Come with me.'

He turned around and retraced his steps, motioning me to walk with him. 'You know, you should not be walking alone here,' he said, 'it is very dangerous for you. You will be robbed, maybe hurt.'

'What about you?' I asked serenely, 'are you not in danger, too?'

He shook his head. 'No, they won't bother me. They know I have nothing. But they will certainly attack you and rob you. It has happened many times before. It happens all the time here.' He paused and pointed ahead. 'There is the internet café,' he said, 'I will introduce you to the owner. He is a friend of mine.'

We entered the internet café and the young man introduced me to a pleasant older black man. There were few other people in the café. Then the young man turned back to me. 'I must leave now but here is my mobile phone number,' he handed me a slip of paper. 'If I can help you in any way, just give me a call and I will come.'

I thanked the young man warmly for his help. He smiled and then said 'Please remember what I said. It is dangerous to walk out there. Do not walk alone.' Then he left.

I turned to the owner of the internet café and explained that I wanted to compose and send a number of emails.

The man indicated one of the terminals lining one wall. 'You can have one hour, Sir. Please use that terminal over there.'

I thanked the man and sat there for the best part of an hour, composing my emails and sending them. When I was finished, I gathered up my papers and rose to go. The owner came over to me. 'Sir,' he said, 'what hotel are you staying at?'

I told him the name. 'It's not very far away,' I said, 'no more than a mile. Thanks for your help.'

He shook his head. 'I am very worried about you. You must not walk alone. You will be robbed, for sure. I am going to come with you to your hotel, to keep you safe. The robbers will not touch you when they see that you are with me.'

'That's very kind,' I responded, 'but I'm sure I'll be fine. Don't worry about me.'

The man was adamant. 'No, you do not understand what happens here. There are gangs of men waiting out there for people like you. It happens all the time. I am coming with you. I am taking you to your hotel.'

We had a pleasant and interesting conversation as we walked to the hotel. The streets were very quiet and I did notice that there were small groups of young black men loitering in the shadows at various places on our journey. However, they showed no interest in us as we walked past. When I arrived back at the hotel, I thanked the man profusely, knowing that he had given me his personal protection in an extremely dangerous situation.

Afterwards, I analysed my feelings about the peculiar experience of that evening. In life, we are warned not to expose ourselves to danger but sometimes we disregard these warnings. I have to admit that my own life experiences have encouraged me to be rather more sceptical of danger than some – thus my rejection of the warnings in this case. In situations like that in Durban, where there is a good deal of violent crime, we are encouraged to think of the indigenous population as dangerous, to be avoided if possible. However, my story presents the opposite. Both the young man I met by chance in the street and the internet café owner were full of love and compassion for me and protected me against the evils in their society with

A Small Piece of Pure Gold

no thought of gain for themselves. Surely that is God at work in them. Surely, they both gave me God's protection, something that I have experienced many times in my life.

17

The Joy of Serving

In 2009, when I resigned from the rather turbulent Treasurer position I had held for a number of years at the Birmingham City Mission, I still felt that I wanted to contribute in a way that would make use of my accountancy and management skills. It was for this reason that I found myself examining job offers on the Chartered Accountant's website. Suddenly I noticed something that had potential interest for me. The "Friends of the Birmingham Museum and Art Gallery" were advertising for someone to fill their Treasurer post on a part-time, voluntary basis. My eyes lit up. I am passionately interested in museums and art galleries. Wherever I go, I am an assiduous visitor of exhibitions of art and artefacts of all kinds. Here was my chance to become an officer of the wonderful Museum and Art Gallery in Birmingham, an establishment that I knew very well and had visited so many times!

The Museum and Art Gallery occupies a rear part of the Birmingham City Council House, an impressive traditional square edifice built around a large open courtyard. This building is a famous landmark that dominates the top of one of Birmingham's central hills. It is quite a long climb up the surrounding roads but, especially if one approaches from the southeast, the unfolding view of the Council House is very striking. Over the years, it became necessary for the Museum to expand and it did so by taking over part of another large public building just behind the Council House and constructing a wide gallery bridge between the two buildings at first-floor height.

The Friends of Birmingham Museum and Art Gallery came into being many decades before in 1931. Its title describes precisely what it is. There is a Chairperson, a Deputy, a Treasurer and 12 Trustees who are voted in for six year periods. There have always been a number of named patrons who have a special interest in the arts and have contributed significantly to the Museum and Art Gallery through the Friends organisation. In addition, the 1200 or so members support the organisation by paying a modest annual subscription. Funds are also further boosted by the organisation of Friends' special events and outings. Moreover, throughout its existence the Friends have benefitted periodically by charitable donations from external charity funding bodies. In turn, the Friends have donated a significant sum to the Museum and Art Gallery every year, to fund development or to commission new works. Today, the Friends employ three staff who work in the Museum and Art Gallery offices; an Administrator, a Bookkeeper and a Subscriptions Clerk.

As I relished the prospect of working there, I remembered the extreme pleasure of being shown around all parts of the huge and very famous Victoria and Albert Museum in London by Helen, my daughter. She was an absolutely wonderful guide because, of course, as an arts graduate who had worked in many different departments of this vast museum, she was very knowledgeable about the exhibits and the details of their acquisition, maintenance and repair. If I became an officer of the Birmingham Museum and Art Gallery, I, too, would become an expert! 'Well, perhaps not an expert like Helen,' I conceded, 'but, hopefully, someone fairly knowledgeable about all that is going on there.'

So, right away, I decided to apply for the post.

In due course I received an invitation to an interview, which would be conducted by several members of the Friends Committee and their professional advisors. On the day I attended, I was shown around the physical environment of the Museum and Art Gallery, introduced to the Friends staff and apprised of the areas of work in which I would be involved. I was also informed that the post would involve attendance at the Museum on at least one day per week. I concluded that the position of Treasurer was well within my experience and abilities. Furthermore, from the limited amount of material I saw, I suspected that the accounts were in need of a good deal of attention!

I enjoyed the interview thoroughly. It was conducted in a professional but friendly way. At the end, I was informed that there were two candidates being considered for the Treasurer post. The interviewing committee said they would let me know the result as soon as it was available.

I was successful! I can still remember the thrill of arriving at the Museum and Art Gallery as a "Officer"! Before long, I had been issued with my official identity card (always to be worn on a chain around my neck!) and I was now free to penetrate to all the "behind the scenes" areas of the Museum and Art Gallery. I also took the opportunity of visiting the various offices in the museum and making the acquaintance of those who worked there. Of course, the Friends staff had periodic contacts with the Museum and Art Gallery staff, especially the Museum Director and the Senior Managers.

Not long after I joined, the Research Department of the museum were working on the very famous and important "Staffordshire Hoard" of treasure which had been found in the Midlands area. This comprised a whole range of ancient items (dated around the 6th Century), many made of pure gold and set with precious stones. The Hoard became a major exhibit for the museum and, subsequently, was loaned out to many other museums. I had some very interesting conversations with the research experts who were working on the artefacts. It was fascinating to see their detailed work of cleaning, analysing and cataloguing. In fact, I was personally involved in obtaining several very special gemstone publications from the United States for the leading expert in the Research Department, to assist him with his research into the precious stones that were set in certain items of the Hoard.

Finally, my officer status also meant that I was invited to the preview of all the special exhibitions that would soon be open to the public. These were always very interesting occasions because, not only did I have the opportunity of closely examining the new or special displays and questioning the experts who were present, but also had the pleasure of meeting a whole range of very interesting people connected with the arts or the administration of the museum. Needless to say, the wine and snacks were very much appreciated, too!

As I had suspected, when I started work I found that the Friends' accounts were in chaos. The previous Treasurer had departed six months before and their accounts had drifted, more or less rudderless, since that time. Furthermore, examination of earlier procedures and records revealed unsatisfactory accounting and a lack of knowledge about Charity Law – an absolute essential, since the Friends are a registered charity. Finally, I found that the Friends' accounts had considerable funds invested in such a way that produced wild fluctuations in the account balance and, in addition, generated unsatisfactory gains. I noted that total control of the investments had for some time been abandoned into the hands of an external investment brokerage firm.

After spending many hours analysing the whole accounting situation, I assembled my findings and reported the facts I had found to the Friends Committee, proposing that I should work with the Friends staff to establish an effective and proper financial structure. Regarding the investment organisation, I suggested that an Independent Financial Advisor be appointed to bring stability and profit to the investments. As the Chair of the Friends Investment Committee (one of the functions of the Treasurer), I would oversee the investment operation to make sure that it was performing optimally. All this was agreed. Of course, the changes took some time to take hold but, in due course, I successfully imposed proper order on the financial structures of the Friends and was able to achieve an essential consistency in the investment profits, too.

Two years later, I was asked by the Museum if I would become the Treasurer of the Birmingham City Council Museum Development Trust, a task which had nothing to do with my position with the Friends. The Museum Trust Accounts had been looked after by the City Council's Finance Department for some years and, since this was completely peripheral to that department's work and responsibilities, the execution of the task had been rightly judged to be inappropriate. I examined the function and the available material, saw where the problems were and accepted the Museum's proposal. I therefore became responsible for the financial operations of the Development Fund, which included the effective investment of the considerable amount of money that was lodged in that fund. I enjoyed this additional work and made sure that the fund was handled profitably.

Not long afterwards, I found myself as a member of yet another specialism – that of a school governor! A church friend had approached me and told me that she was the Chair of the School Governors at a Birmingham primary school. She asked me if I would consider joining her as one of the School Governors. The school was one of the many inner-city primary schools in the city.

A Small Piece of Pure Gold

'But I don't know anything about education or the way schools are run,' I ventured.

'You don't need to have specialised knowledge of schools or education,' she told me, 'you just need to be someone who has an interest in how the next generation is being prepared for adult life.' She paused. 'Mind you,' she added, 'I think your knowledge of money matters would be very relevant. There's a lot of money discussions in the organisation of schools. I think you would find it very interesting.'

Of course I am interested in the progress of the next generation. Furthermore, if my money and business knowledge would be potentially useful, that would make me a worthwhile member of the team.

'What does it involve?' I asked.

'Just two or three meetings per month during term times. We are there to monitor what is going on and to help the Headmaster and his staff to keep the school running effectively.'

'Sounds interesting,' I said, 'count me in.'

It wasn't long before I was visiting the school, which turned out to be quite a surprise in many ways. There were 440 pupils from many different countries across the world. I was told that some of the pupils arrived at the school with little or no knowledge of English; that became the first task of the teachers! Notwithstanding, when inspected, the school received a good OFSTED report. OFSTED is the Government office that inspects and regulates schools and children's services. It is very much to the credit of the Headmaster and his staff that they manage to be so successful with so many foreign children in their classes.

The school organisation was extensive. It employed a total of 93 people (teachers and other staff) and the payroll for the staff was handled by the Local Authority. Nevertheless, there were many other financial matters to attend to within the school and this was dealt with by a Finance Committee which I was immediately invited to join. The school's annual financial allocation totalled an impressive £2,500,000; however, it soon became obvious that there were many charges upon these funds and the money had to be spent very carefully. After I joined the Committee, the school became designated as a "Chequebook School", which gave it control over its own finances.

The Bursar (a member of the Finance Committee) was the business manager of the school. I asked to have a meeting with her to apprise myself of the financial controls, etc., that were in place. Of course, as an accountant, I immediately asked her if I could see the latest Balance Sheet and the Profit and Loss Account.

'We don't have these things here,' the Bursar told me, 'we don't operate that way.'

Although I tried, I never did fully understand how the finances were organised and controlled but, since I was not there to impose standard accounting procedures on the school (or give anyone problems!), I decided to leave the matter in abeyance. However, in view of the large amount of money that flowed into the school account, I suggested to the Bursar that more efficient investment strategies would generate additional cash for the school and said that, since I had direct experience in such matters, I would be very pleased to submit suggestions. I felt sure that any extra money obtained in this way would be most welcome.

With my interest in mathematics, I also asked permission to sit-in on a mathematics class to see how mathematics were being taught in the present day. This was agreed and I had the pleasure of joining a mathematics class and sitting at the back – a reminder of my own schooldays many years before! It was immediately obvious that the teacher was presented with a class of pupils who had widely differing skill levels in mathematics. At the end of the session, I thanked the teacher for allowing me to join her class and asked her how she dealt with the great variation of knowledge/skill that was in front of her.

A Small Piece of Pure Gold

'Well,' she said, 'of course I try to match the tasks I give to the abilities of the pupil but I must bias my attention towards the best so that their development can be optimal.' I felt great admiration for this teacher who was carrying out a very difficult task in a highly skilful way.

I have one final inspiring story to tell. At Christmastime, the school presented a series of nativity plays, all performed by the children. I made sure that I attended every performance and was greatly impressed by the high standard of the traditional Christmas story of Jesus. It was very obvious that the children enjoyed the nativity story greatly and performed it with great enthusiasm and considerable acting skill. They played to packed "houses" on every occasion and the audiences, inevitably comprised of parents and relatives, were obviously spellbound by the quality and enthusiasm of their children's performances. At the end of each performance, the applause was deafening and sustained.

I was particularly enchanted by this reaction to the performances, since I am sure that few of them, children and parents, were actually followers of the Christian faith! For me, this was a touching experience, revealing to me a perfect demonstration of how God wants the world to be. All major faiths teach love and tolerance and this, I thought, was an excellent example.

Meanwhile, there had been a ministerial change at the Four Oaks Church, when Rev David Easton left after his ten year stay. Rev Graham Gee had taken over and looked after the church with kindly and effective enthusiasm until his retirement in 2012.

In 2010, I was asked to take over as Treasurer of the Four Oaks Church. Noting that the accounts were still being operated manually (using hand-written account ledgers, etc.), I immediately started to convert everything to computer (spreadsheet) operations, which greatly simplifies the analyses of financial processes and makes the annual submission of the accounts to the auditors much easier. In addition, I deemed it necessary to adopt the standard "accrual" system of accounting which, crucially, allocates all credits and debits within their correct accounting year to ensure that the accounts always provide an absolutely accurate picture of the Church's finances.

During the five years I served as the Church Treasurer, there were several major financial events, such as the renewal of the kitchen and toilets (as a result of a generous gift) and the refurbishment of the adjacent caretaker's cottage, followed by its conversion to a commercially rented property. Both generated considerable financial activity.

Shortly after I became the Church Treasurer in 2010, I was asked by the daughter of two elderly friends of mine if I would look after their personal finances. Her father, a Local Preacher in the Church for very many years, had succumbed to Alzheimer's Disease and his wife, although still living at home, was increasingly frail and was incapable of looking after the complexities of their finances.

I accepted gladly and it was a great honour to help my old friends with all aspects of their finances until they died in 2014 and 2015. During the years when I was fit and well, I visited them both regularly. They were both wonderful people in my life and I miss them greatly.

In 2015, the progress of my MND prevented me from continuing as the Church Treasurer. I greatly enjoyed my time as Treasurer, because, in addition to using my skill and experience in an efficient way, it brought me into contact with virtually all aspects of the church I love so much. I continue to have contact with the Church's finances as Assistant Treasurer.

There is indeed great joy in serving. In addition to the tasks and responsibilities I have described above, I have always been alert to the needs of others around me. If

A Small Piece of Pure Gold

their needs were complex but within the areas of my own specialisms (e.g. anything associated with finance and / or computers), I was always ready to help to try to solve their problems. However, people often have needs that are much simpler (for instance a lift to and from church), and I have always been alert for these also.

18
Gerald

Gerald was my "big" twin brother, one and a half hours older than me! Physically, we were not "identical twins", although photographs of us as children showed that we were quite similar in appearance. (I could never see the likeness, though!) However, there is no doubt that we were totally dissimilar in character, as the early chapters of this book have chronicled. Once we had left school behind us, our life paths diverged sharply, with Gerald informed that he was to continue working in the family business with my mother and father while I was compulsorily "outsourced" to pursue a professional career in accounting – undoubtedly something of a shock for me at the time!

Although Gerald and I have both lived our adult lives in the Midlands of England with our homes separated physically by less than ten miles, our sharply differing interests and activities meant that our meetings throughout the years tended to be in the "occasional" category. Our shared Christian faith, a very strong component in both of our lives, found us worshipping at different Methodist churches, so we had little contact in that way either, although we did meet periodically at Circuit events. That said, the bond of being twins has always bound us to each other in a deeply fundamental way, perhaps unappreciated at times.

I was well aware that Gerald played a major part in the Stockland Green Church, a place where I had had strong earlier associations. Gerald held the position of Senior Steward at that church and, consequently, was often in the church building or engaged in some way in church business. His wife Anne was also very highly involved with the Church and was well known as a church member who would always step forward to carry out whatever tasks needed to be done; in any church, there are always many tasks that require dedicated attention.

Over the years, Gerald and Anne had participated fully and were often members of the many committees within the church. Such activities are the life-blood of any church. Furthermore, as soon as there were other one-off activities to organise and arrange, they could be depended upon to participate in these initiatives and take a leading role.

Everyone knew Gerald. They knew him for his deep devotion to his faith and the church. They knew him for his generosity and for his unfailing kindness, often delivered within his characteristic and individualistic sense of ironic humour. With Gerald, no matter the subject, there was always a joke to be shared.

Late in 2010, Gerard noticed that he had developed a small swelling near the base of his spine. His doctor examined him and was of the opinion that the lump was "nothing to worry about". Three months later, the lump had developed to become a much more significant swelling in the lumbar region of his lower back. He returned to the doctor who immediately referred him to the Queen Elizabeth Hospital in Birmingham for further diagnosis and tests. The diagnosis suggested a developing cancerous tumour.

In Gerald's case, various treatments appeared to have no significant effect on the tumour and it was finally decided that a surgical operation should be carried out to remove it. This was arranged to take place in June, 2011, by which time the swelling had become much larger and was causing Gerald to be increasingly ill and disabled as well suffering constant, debilitating pain.

For many years, Gerald had also suffered from very high blood pressure and was being treated with a range of medication including the powerful blood-thinning, anti-clotting agent warfarin. When a surgical operation is required, it seems that warfarin treatment must be discontinued. However, for some reason, this did not happen and Gerald was actually anaesthetised and in the operating theatre before this came to light. As a result, it was judged to be too dangerous for the operation to proceed. However, a biopsy (a small tissue sample) of the tumour was taken for analysis. You may imagine that Gerald was far from pleased to discover that his serious operation had been transformed into a mere biopsy!

Nevertheless, the biopsy produced a very unexpected result when the tumour was revealed as a Merkel Cell Carcinoma. This is known to be a highly aggressive type of skin cancer whose tumours grow very rapidly. Furthermore, this type of carcinoma is a very recent discovery, being first identified only in 2008 by medical scientists in the USA. The rarity of this tumour meant that Gerald was visited by many different medical professionals, who wished to see and examine such a new and unusual illness to expand their knowledge and experience.

Further months passed and the tumour continued to grow, with Gerald suffering more and more severe pain and disablement. Eventually, the surgical operation to remove the tumour was carried out in November 2011. A month after the surgery, the post-operative examinations and tests suggested that the operation had been totally successful in removing all the cancerous growth and Gerald was discharged from the hospital as totally cured of his illness. There was of course great rejoicing at this time, both in the family, throughout the church and also in the local business community where Gerald was well-known. The news of this healing was broadcast far and wide.

Sadly, this proved to be a false dawn. Post-operative checks six months later revealed a significant spread of secondary cancers around Gerald's body through his lymph system. By the end of the year, his situation was judged to be terminal and staff from the John Taylor Hospice (the same wonderful organisation that now helps me) now attended him regularly to alleviate his discomfort and suffering. During all this time, although Gerald suffered greatly, he outwardly retained his good-humoured, informal persona. By the middle of 2013, he had become much worse and was often confined to bed. Subsequently, the experts of the John Taylor Hospice helped to ease the last months of his life with constant palliative care, very strong pain-killing medicine and a great deal of love.

Once I was informed of the seriousness of Gerald's condition, I began to visit him regularly each week, re-establishing our old boyhood relationship. Of course we found that we had a great deal to talk about. There were always the comprehensive updates about Gerald's condition – what had been done and said at the hospital, etc. Of course we also recalled the past together, bringing to mind our mother and father in their roles as Methodist Local Preachers and how, in our opinion, they were sometimes rather less than Christian in their parental roles at home! However, with the benefit of maturity, we did agree that such variations within family life are likely to be quite common. We also remembered how we were required to work in the family business without ever being paid. As slaves, we used to say!

Then there were many conversations about Methodist Church matters, past, present and future. Even although we attended different churches, my previous association with Gerald's church at Stockland Green meant that I knew many members of the congregation who attended there. Every church is a microcosm of activity and it was always interesting to hear the latest goings-on! In turn, I was able to update Gerald on the situation at my church in Four Oaks. Furthermore, any time we ran out of current stories to tell, there was always a plethora of stories to recall from the past!

Of course I had many Museum and Art Gallery stories to tell, not only about the many interesting exhibits and special exhibitions that were presented to the public but also the details of the internal politics that always rage within any substantial organisation. During my tenure there, there were a number of changes to senior staff, including several new Museum Directors. It was always fascinating to "get to know" the new incumbents and find out what their particular viewpoints were (inevitably very different from their predecessors!). Then, when I became a school governor, I was able to tell Gerald many stories about the machinations of that environment, too, as well as the delightful experiences I had with the pupils there.

There was some business talk as well, although I have to say that Gerald gave business matters a very much lower priority in his life that I had done in mine. Nevertheless, we had something of a shared interest in his wholesale marketing business (originally set up by my father many years before), because I had been his accountant for a number of years previously. When I started to look after the finance of his business, all financial records were laboriously and inefficiently hand-written. I explained to Gerald that I would need to convert future accounts to simple computer operations and that he must learn how to input his business figures into the spreadsheets that I would set up. This proved to be quite a task, since Gerald was not interested in computers – that is, until he found out that there were "Bridge" game programs he could access! For many years, Gerald had been an excellent bridge player, so skilled that he taught the game as a lecturer at college classes.

After Gerald was informed that he was free from cancer, he decided that the time had come to dispose of his wholesale business operations along with the rented properties that also occupied the extensive Nechells site. He informed me that he intended to sell everything to a friend who was interested in taking it all over. A price had already been agreed, he said. When he revealed what the price was, I immediately advised him that the sum appeared to be far too low. I recommended strongly (as his accountant) that he should have the business and the associated properties professionally valued. This would provide him with a valid market price for all his assets, I said. I pointed out that a realistic, market price would be fair to all parties, both buyer and seller. Gerald was totally uninterested in my recommendation and insisted that he would go ahead with his friend at the agreed (in my opinion, low) price. In due course, this is exactly what he did.

I have often said that Gerald was uninterested in the tenets of business (e.g. making a profit!) – his casual and kindly commercial dealings over the years had proven that amply. There is no doubt that he was a loving and very generous man whose interests were directed almost solely at and through the church.

During 2012, I had become interested in the recent history of the South Asia region, particularly in the totally nefarious and incomprehensible actions of the Cambodian dictator, Pol Pot, who was the leader of the infamous Khmer Rouge force in the latter part of the 20th Century. As history records, Pol Pot was responsible for an inexplicable and intensely cruel genocide of his own people during a four year period from 1975 to 1979. There are many accounts and analyses of the dreadful acts that took place every day.

As there are many other unique sights and antiquities within that region, I decided to take a short break from the routine of my home life and join a whistle-stop holiday tour early in 2013, covering parts of Thailand, Laos and Cambodia; this would include the infamous "Killing Fields" surrounding Phnom Penh in Cambodia. Of course I was concerned about what may happen to Gerald while I was absent. However, the tour was scheduled to last just 17 days and I asked Anne, Gerald's wife, to contact me by email if Gerald's condition worsened markedly. I would then return home immediately, I told her.

Apart from my visit to the Cambodian Killing Fields, which will remain in my memory for the rest of my life, I had many other unique experiences during the tour of these three countries, starting with the fact that the train that would transport me on a long 13 hour journey from Bangkok to the borders of Laos broke down before it had moved an inch from the Bangkok railway station. It took five hours to find another engine that worked! In due course, eventually, we did arrive in Vientiane, the capitol of Laos.

Other memories of the tour include a two day excursion along the mighty Mekong River in Laos, with a visit to the Pak Ou caves, which are dramatically filled with thousands of Buddha figures. Then, after a flight to Cambodia, there were visits to the ancient sites around Angkor Wat, famous as the largest temple complex in the world and the centre of an incredibly sophisticated civilisation 1,500 years ago.

Finally, a coach took us to Phnom Penh, location of the Cambodian genocide carried out by Pol Pot and his Khmer Rouge forces during 1975-79. The Killing Fields comprise a large number of sites around Phnom Penh that contain the mass graves of up to three million Cambodian people (40% of the population of Cambodia at the time). The history of what happened is well documented and it tells a story of immense cruelty and what can only be described as bestial behaviour by Khmer Rouge forces, who were mostly uneducated young peasants, both male and female, specially recruited by Pol Pot for this task.

In 1979, after four years of genocide operations, Vietnam attacked Cambodia and the Khmer Rouge forces were quickly defeated. Pol Pot fled to a jungle area near the Thailand border and, incredibly, continued to "rule" the remnants of the Khmer Rouge until his death in 1998, almost 20 years later! While still alive, he always denied that he had been responsible for the 1975-79 genocide. His conscience was clear, he said and he blamed his unruly, "overenthusiastic" forces for the extensive killings. Although Pol Pot has been convicted of genocide "in absentia" in the Cambodian Courts, he was never arrested and punished for this absolutely heinous crime.

A Genocide Museum has been set up in Phnom Penh, in the Tuol Sleng School that Pol Pot turned into a dreadful prison and interrogation centre in 1974. Our tour included a comprehensive visit there. I can only say that the information and exhibits in the museum were extremely disturbing and absolutely horrific, undoubtedly amounting to a wholly depressing example of man's inhumanity to man. 20,000 Cambodian people were killed in that place, men, women and children of all ages, including babies. There were just seven survivors and I had the privilege of meeting one of them and buying the book that he had written about his experiences.

This man, Bou Meng, was arrested with his wife and was imprisoned, beaten, starved and tortured. Then, Pol Pot discovered that he was a professional artist and ordered that he should be released so that he could paint many portraits of the "Great Man". During the four year period of the genocide, while millions of innocent people died, Bou Meng painted hundreds of portraits of Pol Pot and was kept alive only for that reason. Had he refused at any time, there is no doubt he would have been killed immediately, probably after severe torture. His wife did not survive the prison and he never knew what happened to her.

When I spoke to him, I could see clearly the pain and bewilderment in his eyes.

After I returned to the UK, I recommenced my regular weekly visits to Gerald. His condition continued to deteriorate but, for as long as he could, he forced himself to continue all his normal activities associated with the church. Although he was suffering crippling disablement and pain, Gerald fought to maintain his old, ironically cheerful self and most of his church friends never suspected the degree of his incapacitation and suffering. At that time, I was often astonished at the depth of his courage and I still consider him one of the bravest men I have ever known.

By June 2013, even Gerald had to capitulate to his disease. For some time, he had needed to resort to doses of morphine medication to control his pain. Now he needed morphine routinely, delivered intravenously from a pump. As a result, he became increasingly disorientated and, by the end of summer, stopped speaking. When I visited him, all he wished to do was hold my hand, which he did with a surprisingly firm grip. On one occasion, when it was time for me to leave, Gerald would not let go! It took me some time to extricate my hand. I remember that my nephew Graham (my sister Angela's son) was visiting with me on that day and helped me to persuade Gerald to finally loosen his grip.

During the summer months, a change of minister was taking place at Stockland Green Methodist Church. This usually results in a "ministerial gap" in July and August, while the leaving minister takes his summer holidays and is involved with moving to his new location. The new minister does not take over the post until 1st September and, normally, is not seen until then. However, when the new minister, Rev. Paul Dunstan, heard of Gerald's serious

A Small Piece of Pure Gold

illness, he began to visit him and the two formed a warm and positive relationship. I understood that they sometimes drank beer together! I think this was a wonderful and generous act of compassion by Paul Dunstan and I know it was greatly appreciated by Gerald and Anne.

On the 22nd of September 2013, I was visiting Gerald as usual, on this occasion accompanied by my daughter Helen. Gerald had always been Helen's favourite uncle! Of course Gerald was holding my hand but there was little other communication between us. Mostly, he was near unconsciousness. We all knew that the end was not far off. When the time came for us to leave, I extricated my hand from his and we said our goodbyes. Half an hour later, Anne phoned to say that he had just died, just slipped away while she was with him. Helen and I returned immediately to help and support Anne. In the following days, I supported Anne as she dealt with all the procedures and arrangements that follow a death. We had all known that Gerald had very little time left but the death of a loved one is always a tremendous shock when it comes.

Gerald had expressed a clear wish for cremation after death and was cremated at Sutton Coldfield Crematorium. The chapel was filled to capacity. At the Service of Thanksgiving that followed the cremation, Stockland Green Methodist Church was filled to overflowing, with around 200 people present. As well as the family, there were many friends, not only from the Stockland Green Church but from many other Methodist churches in the Birmingham District, as well as many others who had known Gerald through links with his business and other activities. The funeral and thanksgiving service were conducted by Rev. Paul Dunstan, who had come to know Gerald and his family very well.

In a short address of beautiful, inspirational words, Paul Dunstan reminded the congregation that they were present to celebrate Gerald's life and to bring their thanks and memories of his devoted service to God. In saying that Gerald was now in the hands of God, he spoke these words:

'There is no safer place to be than in the hands of the Heavenly Living Father, who was with Gerald throughout his life.' Wonderful and very comforting words for Gerald's loved ones.

He also read a short passage from the First Epistle of Peter (1Pet 1:3-4) which speaks of the inheritance awaiting every Christian in Heaven as a result of the sacrifice of our Lord Jesus Christ.

It is customary at Thanksgiving Services for several relatives and friends of the deceased to deliver "eulogies" – which is an impressive and formal word to describe a number of loving and affectionate anecdotes that pay tribute to the departed. In addition, the eulogies often include significant elements of humour. In my experience of thanksgiving services, I would say there are often two or three eulogies; in Gerald's case, there were seven!

As Gerald's twin brother, I was the first to speak. I started by informing everyone that the hymns for the service had been chosen by Gerald, himself. Obviously, he did not want to leave anything to chance! I then read out a letter on behalf of my sister Angela, who was in New Zealand and unable to be present. It was a letter to Gerald, in which she told him that he had always been "an easy person to love" and that he always had a "big heart". She recalled happy family times and how Gerald always helped her when she was sad for any reason. She was especially grateful that her son, Graham, who had been brought up in New Zealand and had never met Gerald, was able to come to England earlier in the year and had been able to form a family relationship with his uncle before he died.

My own tribute to Gerald, took the form of three statements about different parts of his life.

The first referred to a recurring event when we were both at school, when I, wishing to visit the toilet, was nevertheless too embarrassed to ask the teacher. Observing this,

Gerald would raise his hand and make the request for me! (I have already told this story in Chapter 3 of this book.) However, the point is, I continued in my address, Gerald then reminded me of this recurring scene many times during our lives, often embarrassing me in the presence of others who did not know the story!

The second referred to Gerald's kindness and generosity to all – extending even to business customers who did not pay for the goods and services he had provided! As a businessman, it seems that he was uninterested in the normal rules of commerce and profit. It is clear he had a different focus on life.

In my final comment, I referred to the aggressive cancer that had finally taken him, after a prolonged struggle with pain and disablement. I said: 'I have never known a more brave man. He concealed his pain so well that most of his friends would not have known that anything was wrong. I am so very proud of him.'

I then finished with a Bible reading from John's Gospel, Chapter 14.

My "eulogy" was then followed by six more, all paying warm tributes to Gerald.

At the beginning of this chapter, I mentioned how the life paths of Gerald and me started to diverge from our mid-teenage years. Although, for a number of years, I still lived in the same house as my brother and the family, essentially I had become detached from the others. Yet, Gerald and I were not only brothers, we were twins — I believe this to be an unbreakable bond.

I did feel Gerald's death deeply and, in the following months, I attributed my sense of unease and a growing physical depletion to a deep sense of grief within me. I have no doubt that the sense of grieving was there; unfortunately, so was the beginning of motor neurone disease.

19

July, 2015

Time is infinitely elastic. It passes quickly and slowly. Eight whole months of metered time has passed since I left you, the reader, in November 2014 at page 16 of this book. This was at the end of Chapter 1, which chronicled the onset, diagnosis and rapid development of my MND. However, in a timespan of a different dimension, seventy years of my life have also been projected across the pages of Chapter 2 to Chapter 18.

To bring the book to a close, this final chapter brings you up to date and offers my concluding thoughts on all the joys, the sorrows and the continuum that joins these two extremes, to express the wholeness of my life.

It is fair to say that by the end of November 2014 I was sinking fast. My MND had imposed great changes upon my body. I was finding it increasingly difficult to breathe, my sleep at night was extremely fitful and I had lost my appetite for food or drink. My friends and family have since told me that they doubted whether I would still be alive at Christmastime. I remember finding it impossible to concentrate when Jack and I were starting our initial sessions on the content of this book. Jack has told me that

I often fell asleep at that time, sometimes in mid-sentence. I remember I was permanently exhausted and increasingly weak. In fact, I was dying.

In the previous months when my condition was rather better, there had been talk of various aids to help me with the worsening symptoms of my condition. I was advised that a night-time "breathing machine" would be able to help me with my sleep; also, that a fully adjustable hospital-type bed would provide me with the best possible sleep environment. In addition, I should agree to be fitted with a feeding tube (directly into my stomach) as soon as possible because the progress of my MND meant that I would soon be unable to swallow. Thereafter, this direct method of feeding would be the only way for me to acquire nutrition, I was told. I remember reacting rather negatively to this suggestion, because it seemed to be such a radical and alien step to take when I wasn't experiencing any swallowing problems at that time.

In due course, all these aids were provided and there is no doubt that they saved my life. I wore the mask of the breathing machine every night and this, coupled with the very comfortable hospital bed, gave me nights of blissfully uninterrupted sleep. I soon found that my appetite for food and drink had returned. Notwithstanding my amazing improvement, I capitulated and had the surgical operation to install the feeding tube (a PEG) into my stomach. I did have a problem with it at first, because it was very painful and required further adjustment at the hospital. Since then it has functioned satisfactorily. The bags of liquid food that I require are ingested at night when I am asleep.

Because I could no longer climb the stairs of my house, my bedroom had to be relocated downstairs and I had a spacious study room converted into an attractive bedroom. Likewise, my main bathroom now had to be downstairs and my downstairs bathroom has become a fully-fitted wet room with a full range of aids that make it possible for me to look after all my bathing needs. The upstairs rooms of my house have become permanent guest rooms!

The John Taylor Hospice has also provided special furniture to suit my new life, such as a very comfortable electric armchair which can lift me up, a three-wheeled walking frame to help me move around safely and a whole range of other aids to compensate for the increasing weakness of my limbs. Additional breathing equipment has been provided for daytime use and to deal with coughing and throat congestion situations. I also have a lightweight wheelchair for outdoor excursions, with the future prospect of an electric wheelchair and a ramp from my front door to turn me into a more independent traveller. Meanwhile, because a sturdy wheelchair ramp has already been installed at my back door, I can now be wheeled into my wonderful garden. Here, I rejoice in the fresh air outside and find an increasing fascination with all the wonderful things in nature that surround me. Now, I have more time to "stand and stare" and that is exactly what I do! With the much slower pace of my life, I am seeing what I have missed for so many years.

In addition to my breathing difficulties, the weakening of my lung muscles has continued to diminish my voice. Unfortunately, my days of shouting are definitely over! When I speak, people often ask me to repeat my words, which can be frustrating. Articulation of more complex words continues to be difficult, too. However, I am grateful that people understand my problems and are patient with me.

I have had to learn lessons the hard way! In my house, twice I have attempted to pick up an object from the floor and have fallen down, only to find that I no longer have the strength to regain my feet. On the first occasion I was able to squirm along the floor to my kitchen and make use of a chair to clamber upright. On the second occasion (by this time I was even weaker), I was lucky enough to have my trusty mobile phone with me and was able to obtain help in that way. Now I wear an alarm button designed precisely for such emergencies. And – I have learned – I don't attempt to pick things up from the floor!

Nevertheless, there is one piece of good news to report! The MND has not affected my swallowing and I am still able to eat food normally. This is of course a great bonus. However, my medical experts recommend that I should continue to supplement what I eat by means of the PEG stomach tube, to ensure that I continue to be fortified by the best possible diet.

I am so fortunate to have an almost continuous succession of personal visitors and callers on my telephone. In addition, many of my friends take me out to places where I can meet other people and this is always very enjoyable. Diane remains a loving tower of strength and I feel so privileged to know such a wonderfully caring person. All the members of my family, especially Helen, Paul and his wife Natacha do so much for me and show me endless love.

When Rev. Graham Gee retired in 2012, the Four Oaks Church was blessed with the arrival of two ministers, albeit instructed to look after three churches in the Circuit. (Methodist ministers usually have responsibility for more than one church.) Our new minister was Rev. John Rowe, very ably assisted by his wife, Deacon Liz Rowe. They are a delightful and truly inspiring couple who have lifted our church in so many ways. God's love blazes from them both, yet that love is so often projected in the joy of laughter. Since my illness, John and Liz Rowe have supported me assiduously, visiting me often and taking me to church services in my wheelchair. More importantly, however, they sustained me and immeasurably strengthened my faith in God, through a very special visit to the Holy Land.

I was privileged to join John and Liz Rowe and a group of other Christians on a visit to the Holy Land in March 2014, just before my MND manifested itself positively.

I know that I have already described visits to the Holy Land in this book and I do not intend to repeat myself. However, this visit to the Holy Land under the leadership of the Rowes was such an exceptional experience for me that I must mention it here.

The visit proved to be one of the most spiritual experiences of my life, a pilgrimage like no other. John and Liz Rowe guided our group through a series of visits, at the same time both logical and spiritual, and surely transported us to an awareness of God in a way that I have never before experienced. I can only describe it thus:

To be intensely aware of walking in the footsteps of Jesus Christ and those of St. Paul was truly breath-taking.

To follow the circuitous Via Dolorosa and pause at the Stations of the Cross, traditionally the way that Jesus Christ walked while carrying the Cross upon which he was crucified at Golgotha, and contemplate his pain at each step.

To take the Sacrament of Holy Communion beside the lake and feel the presence of Jesus.

To listen to John Rowe's readings from God's Word and his beautiful prayers as we sailed serenely on the Sea of Galilee, just as Jesus had done.

To be blessed by John Rowe in the waters of the River Jordan and to contemplate the baptism of Jesus by John the Baptist over 2,000 years ago.

To pray by the Pool of Bethsaida in a spirit of intercession, thinking of the people back home.

I found all these events were spiritual experiences of cataclysmic intensity, hugely meaningful for me. It was ten days of pure heaven and acted to deepen my faith in God immeasurably; perhaps it was to prepare me for what was to come; I do not know.

I am so grateful to John and Liz, who are truly God's people in every way.

These days, I also have more time to contemplate my spiritual development. Since I was a teenager, I have always felt close to God and I now think that the joys and tragedies in my life acted to bring me even closer to Him each time. Throughout my life, it has always been a great delight to me to recognise other Christians, whether I meet them personally or see them from afar. It is truly wonderful to see God at work in others.

My MND, while restricting me physically, has, in fact, expanded me in other ways. I feel so blessed to have come in contact with all my medical carers at the Queen Elizabeth Hospital, the John Taylor Hospice and in other places, too. These are truly wonderful people, giving everything they have, and giving it with a love that only God can provide.

I also want to say that my life, now so closely bound up with MND, engenders absolutely no negative thoughts in me. In fact, the reverse is true. In a strange way, I now feel blessed and think of each day as a special bonus to be used and enjoyed – and there is no better way to do so than to be alive to God's presence and be ready to do his work. I say to everyone; offer yourself to God and he will use you, no matter where you are, how you are or whatever your situation.

Finally, I would sum things up like this. The last nine months, during which time this book has grown to completion, has been a time of intense joy and fulfilment for me. My author friend Jack has listened carefully to every word I have spoken and then gone beyond the paucity of their meaning to reach into the truth of my soul. I have been totally honest about my actions and thoughts throughout my life and Jack's searching questions have acted to unlock many other long-forgotten nuances of memory too. What has been written by him really does represent the joy and sorrows of my life and all the thoughts and experiences in the rainbow spectrum between.

July, 2015

Looking back, I see my life as a rich tapestry of learning experiences, with my joys and sorrows representing the intense peaks and troughs of that amazing continuum. I feel so very privileged to have met so many good people, not only in my own country but in other areas of the world. God has certainly created mankind finely and it is so obvious that his goodness pervades all. It is a great joy to have met so many Godly people. The world is such a wonderful place and I am so grateful that I was able to expand my own knowledge by experiencing cultures and philosophies outside my own.

I also want to emphasise how my MND has generated only a very few negatives in my life. I am sad that I cannot help people as I used to do, for I have always considered this to be one of the purposes in my life – and I must admit to finding it hard to accept help from others. Feelings of independence are still strong but the flesh is weakening! I shall also miss seeing my grandchildren growing up – but who knows what I will be able to witness in the life hereafter? That said, my MND has also been a surprising source of joy because I have so many new and wonderful friends who seek out my company and are happy to spend time with me. In fact, everyone talks to me and share their own joys and sorrows!

In conclusion, I thank God for his loving grace that granted me faith in the Lord Jesus Christ as my personal Saviour, through the gift of the Holy Spirit. My faith has enabled me to live a wonderful life of service to Him.

I have absolutely no worries or concerns. My feelings are constantly at peace and I have no fear of the death I know is coming. Meanwhile, as long as I live, I will continue to treat each day as a new and wonderful experience.

Captions for photos on next pages

page 238 top: the twins John and Gerald's 60th birthday party (2004) with their other siblings, from left to right: Gerald, David, Angela, John, Peter.

page 238 bottom: John Nodding teaching his eldest son Paul some photography skills (back garden of home in Birmingham Road) 1980.

page 239 top: a family holiday in Devon c 1986; from left, Helen, Paul, Mark, John.

page 239 bottom: Maureen and John on an evening out with friends c. 1964, before they were married.